Hope you Enjoy the
Book.

your Friend
Don
Miller

Your
Exceptional
Life
Begins Now

Life is priceless... Make yours count!

MARYANNA YOUNG & KIM FLETCHER

with 24 Co-Authors

ALOHA PUBLISHING

Your Exceptional Life Begins Now
By Maryanna Young and Kim Fletcher

Copyright © 2005

Published by:
Aloha Publishing
1810 W State Street, Suite 431
Boise, ID 83702
208 447 9036
alohabookcompany@aol.com
www.Your ExceptionalLifeBeginsNow.com

Cover and Interior by NZ Graphics, www.nzgraphics.com

ISBN: 0976264234

13 digit ISBN: 978-0-9762642-3-1

Library of Congress Control Number: 2005909965

If you find typographical errors in this book, we would love to know about them for further editions. Please email us at alohabookcompany@aol.com. They serve a purpose. Some people actually enjoy looking for them and we aim to please as many people as possible.

This book is available at www.YourExceptionalLifeBeginsNow.com OR www.DontMissYourBoat.com. They are also available at websites of the Co-Authors, retail locations throughout the US and Canada, and through online retailers including Amazon.com.

Quantity discounts are available by calling SparkWeb Fulfillment at 208 376 1874 or online at www.YourExceptionalLifeBeginsNow.com

Retail Price
$14.95 USA
$19.95 Canada

First Printing 2006

DEDICATED TO...

Ernest & Dorsie Hartley ...
Your impact and influence shaped me.
Your authentic faith still guides my every step.

Kim Fletcher

My twenty nieces and nephews...
Angela, Janette, Sarah, Elizabeth, Gabrielle,
Elysse, Josiah, Liberty, Jacob, Mercy, Joel, Justin,
Anne Marie, Caleb, Joshua, Samuel,
Heidi, Adam, Serenity, and Arielle.
You inspire me by
choosing to live exceptional lives.
Each one of you is God's gift to me.

Maryanna Young

Your Exceptional Life Begins Now
~ Table of Contents ~

INTRODUCTION

IT CANNOT be argued that we are living in one of the most affluent time periods in history. Those of us living in America enjoy life in one of the world's richest countries. Yet there seems to be a tremendous disconnect between the riches we have and the perspective with which many people approach life. Many of us appear more focused on what we want or do not have, failing to grasp all that we already possess.

Consumed with our day to day routines, many of us seem to have difficulty embracing an attitude of abundance. Being truly wealthy and failing to realize it is one of the most prevalent forms of poverty today and it threatens to rob us of the ability to look forward with clarity, hope and passion.

At the time that this book was being completed, Hurricane Katrina, one of the largest natural disasters in American history, devastated New Orleans. I was honored to become part of the large community of individuals who came alongside the survivors in the days following the storm. My own life perspective was challenged by a beautiful woman who was a resident at the shelter where I was serving. She escaped out of the flood waters with her life, her son and a few personal belongings that could easily be held in one small bag. She expressed to me one day that she was tired of hearing many of the other survivors say that they had lost everything. She went on to say, "I have my life, my faith and my son. **I haven't lost everything … I have everything!**"

Wow, now there's is a radical perspective. Her statement was not an attitude of denial but a deep expression of gratitude for the truly important in life.

What would happen in each of our lives today if we were to reassess the truly important and make a determined effort to focus with gratitude on all we have? This woman found new meaning and value in what remained and she was determined to encourage others with her message of hope. That is the radical result of a positive perspective.

Like the survivors of Hurricane Katrina, each of us has known our own personal and professional devastation. However, think with me for a moment. How would every day change if you began taking the unique perspective of my friend, choosing to see what has been lost or never obtained as an opportunity to be grateful for all that already IS?!

Your Exceptional Life Begins Now offers a cultural challenge ... a call to embrace a radical new perspective. Your 'exceptional life' is your true wealth. This life is obtained as we become intentional about creating great life experiences, determine to be on the lookout for exceptional moments, express gratitude for the smallest gifts, and commit to authentic faith and a life of positive influence.

Your exceptional life is waiting... Stop searching and start living!

Kim Fletcher

You want ME to write about an Exceptional Life?

TINA SWANSON BROOKES

"The journey itself will change you forever –
not only your priorities, but your passions.
It alters not only your direction, but your desires.
It transforms not only your actions, but your values.
It makes you just like Christ and unlike anyone else.
It is nothing less than leaving the fake for the real."
– Erwin Raphael McManus

"EXCEPTIONAL LIFE?!! Exceptional?!! I'm struggling just to have a life. You know, a boring, mundane, ordinary life where I do as little harm as possible to the people I love. A life where I barely get all the 'necessaries' done like kissing my husband and children, saying my prayers, calling friends, going to work, and clearing a path through the house. It's all I can do to have a life, and now you expect me to make it exceptional?!! Are you crazy?!!"

After all, what do I know about an exceptional life? Now, I am an expert on the chaotic on-the-run-rest-only-when-you-collapse life. I know that! I understand that I fall far short of my Susie Homemaker house where the motto is "There's a place for everything and everything in its place." In reality, the motto for our home is "Finders Keepers!"

Anyway, with my less than tidy life, what can I say about an exceptional life? Well, I've been studying on that.

"Beauty is in the Eye of the Beholder." You and I may not be thinking the same thing when we say 'exceptional life.' For instance, a model may think an exceptional life is making it to super model status or maintaining her size zero figure well into her forties. I can tell you right now, if that was my idea of an exceptional life, I'd have

Believe me, if I'm going to have an exceptional life, it has to be do-able!

to be shot and put out of my misery! This body has never seen a size zero and I work hard to maintain my 'I've had three children and I'm not expecting number four' figure. Believe me, if I'm going to have an exceptional life, it has to be do-able! So first decide what is important to you. Then, start learning from people around you that live out those values. There's no reason to re-invent the wheel!

Here's what I learned from watching the heroes in my life:

"It's all about me!" attitudes have to go! Replace them with "It's all about you!" attitudes. People I most admire are others-focused. They are more concerned about the welfare of those around them than climbing the ladder of success. They are part of life's solutions to problems, not always stirring-the-pot to keep trouble brewing. (Guess that means soap operas are out of the question as exceptional life models!) Seriously, the people I am talking about are the kind of people that change their world one person at a time. Not THE world perhaps, but THEIR world. Knowing them makes a difference in your life.

My heroes are motivated by the force bigger than themselves, God. They are passionate people. Their lives reflect a dedicated-purpose-goal-ministry mentality. They are not at the mercy of life, tossing them to and fro on the sea of emotions. Rather, they look to God to command their ship through troubled waters. They have a clear idea of who they are and how they want to be. Their actions are determined by their deeply anchored beliefs in Christ.

The power of God in their lives drives them to be mentors. They grow other people just like a gardener grows plants. Their energies, efforts, and resources aren't exhausted on THINGS, but on PEOPLE. They are intentional about leaving their mark on the hearts of people they raise, teach, supervise, counsel, or casually meet in the line at the grocery store. They value people and have a strong desire for others to live exceptional lives.

My heroes have paid their dues. They don't have exceptional lives because life has been easy. To the contrary, their exceptional lives have often come as the result of "Black Hole Experiences." That's what I call it when a tragedy strikes and suddenly you are thrust into a black hole. At that instant, there is no past and no future. There is only the heart-breaking reality of loss. Black Hole Experiences have the power to plummet people into the depths of despair and depression. They can send the brightest and best running to drugs and alcohol for comfort. These are the types of experiences that can destroy lives. Yet somehow my heroes came through their Black Hole Experiences stronger, wiser, and rooted even deeper in their faith. I have watched them hold on to their beliefs like life preservers. They refused to let life beat them down. They live an exceptional life because they CHOOSE to live an exceptional life. They are COMMITTED to living an exceptional life. Not because it is easy or in vogue. But because they have determined an exceptional life built on faith in Christ is worth fighting for day after day, every day!

When I think about it, maybe, just maybe, people live exceptional lives out of sheer determination to be true to their faith. And if that's so, maybe even I can live an exceptional life. I can be pretty stubborn myself sometimes. Watch out world! My exceptional life begins now. Want to join me?

Tina Swanson Brookes
bedynamic@yahoo.com

Make it a Million Dollar Day

MARYANNA YOUNG

MY GRANDMOTHER, Mary Oppel, was a driving force in my life. She was a beautiful, funny, athletic, straight-to-the-point woman. A mix of elegance and faith, she read her Bible daily and never left the house without looking as if she was going out to a special event. The only exception was when she was going out to walk or do some other form of exercise. Even then she was highly color coordinated and had her hair fixed just perfectly. She was spontaneous and cool. Grandma was the person that children, teenagers and her own peers loved to be around. At the age of 84, she ran and walked to finish a 5K (3.1 miles) in just under 30 minutes. She was truly an amazing woman and took the meaning of grace, beauty and strength to new levels for me in my young adulthood. I am sure many of you have had a person in your life that you have admired in a similar way.

Grandma Mary lived with me in my home the last five years of her life. It was a few years after the death of my grandfather, her husband of 59 years. It wasn't that she couldn't live alone, she just loved people and I think that the thought of having more people around appealed to her. She was healthy despite having quadruple bypass surgery, and she wanted to be able to travel between grandchildren and visit friends in various parts of the world. It was in those five years that we had the greatest times of our lives together. However, as a very driven young professional at that time in my life, work often came before family, friends and most everything in my life. I have some regret that I didn't stop and enjoy the moments more.

Then something happened that I never saw coming. It was so unexpected that it did not even seem real when it did happen. Grandma Mary passed away from a brain aneurysm. It happened suddenly. Her final day was spent happily doing her daily routine from her short walk in the neighborhood to making dinner. Days before, she had told me "I feel so good, I'm sure that I will live another ten years." Her death rocked my world.

Somewhere in life we have each had that circumstance that has spun our world upside down.

You don't know what to think. You are numb. You wish that you could turn back time to a far less painful point. It causes you to take stock of most everything that you do.

Although it was the life of my grandmother that impacted me daily, it was upon her death that I was completely changed. It was the realization of the impact that one person could make on your life. At that *moment of truth* I really began to understand the purpose for our lives and the impact that we can each make on each other.

I remember pleading with God, "If I could have one more day with Grandma, I would pay a million dollars. I didn't know that the days that we had together were going to be the last ones."

Just as the words came out of my mouth, I remember this statement coming to me, "Don't worry, your Grandma is with Me and you can live million dollar days with the people all around you now."

That understanding greatly changed my life. I restructured my work completely, began putting time and energy into significant relationships and began living each day as if it was worth a million dollars. Simply put, I committed daily to ask God to give me the grace to laugh more, hug more, forgive more, and allow His love to flow through me to others. I see taking time for weekends out or short vacations with the people I love as a wonderful asset. They are more important than any project that I might be called on to be a part of...regardless of the honor or prestige that might be attached to it.

Then something happened that I never saw coming. It was so unexpected that it did not even seem real when it did happen.

I have also come to realize that you can choose to live an exceptional life among any circumstances. Difficult circumstances and challenges beyond what we can comprehend do enter our lives. I also recognized that items on a To Do List and Schedule Reminders on Outlook will always be there but I can choose to focus on the small moments and memories that make up my Million Dollar Days.

Seizing Million Dollar Days might simply mean showing up at your child's school unexpectedly or asking your work team to take up slack so that you can attend a sporting event or birthday party for a family member, spouse or friend. Think about who might cherish the moments of a Million Dollar Day if you were intentional about creating them often.

It might mean that you buy a plane ticket to see someone who has greatly touched your life to let them know that being in your life is priceless. It could also mean stepping out and acting in kindness for someone you might never see beyond that moment. It can be as simple as dropping a card to someone with words that can change their perspective for a day, a month or even a lifetime.

Our lives were meant to have a positive ripple effect. Changing someone's viewpoint by your kindness, your time and sharing a part of you in a meaningful way may impact their family, their co-workers and how they interact in their community.

What daily reminder can you create that will allow you to choose to live every day as a "Million Dollar Day?" You don't have to have a million dollars in the bank, have a million dollar home, or know anyone that does. The gift of time, the gift of the everyday, is available to you. Make today, and every day, a "Million Dollar Day."

Maryanna Young
Personal Value Coaching
Life and Business Coach, Speaker, Author and Friend
"Helping ordinary people achieve extraordinary dreams"
www.personalvaluecoaching.com
personalvalue@aol.com

Attitude Is Everything!

STACY JAMES

MY LIFE was planned out. I would graduate from college in a year, earn my black belt, join a certain ministry, and spend the summer on a missions project. Just when we have plans, it is amazing how they can change…literally in an instant.

What happened next, I remember distinctly. It was my Journalism class project. I had the idea to navigate my college campus in a wheelchair and write about handicap accessibility for our school newspaper. Unfortunately, I had a wrong attitude toward people in wheelchairs. I thought, "Why change the world for such a small part of the population?" But that Friday I put myself in a friend's wheelchair for the day, and wheeled to my classes, the cafeteria, and in and out of restrooms. I typed my story and laid it on my desk to hand in on Monday. The next day my life changed forever.

It was the first Saturday in June – our annual kick-off-the-summer pool party in my friend's backyard. Forty of us gathered for a fun get together before heading off in our various directions for the summer. We got in the shallow end of the pool, and I climbed on my friend's shoulders. I started losing my balance, so I dove toward the deep end of the pool. Suddenly, my head slammed on the bottom and my body went completely limp.

I lay facedown, paralyzed. "Help!" I wanted to yell. "I can't move! God, help me!" I prayed.

When I didn't think I could hold my breath any longer, someone grabbed my waist and brought me to the top. I gasped for air. They placed me on the side of the pool, and I could barely feel or move my body. I was terrified.

An ambulance rushed me to the hospital and into the Emergency Room. I was put through an MRI, which showed a broken neck in three places. The neurosurgeon cut my hair on each side, and placed my head in a steel clamp. Nurses stuck in IV's, heart monitors, and tubes down my nose and throat. Later, a steel black halo was screwed into my skull, and the doctors told my single mother I would never walk again.

My summer mission and all my well set-in-place life plans had suddenly changed. Now I lay paralyzed from the neck down in intensive care. I remember lying there examining my lifeless hands that once played piano, guitar, and twirled a baton. Nurses waited on me, while family and friends visited and prayed.

I didn't know it at the time, but my mom refused to believe the doctor's grim prognosis, and she never told me what they said. "I didn't raise a daughter for nineteen years to have her lay in bed the rest of her life," she said. She was committed to me, camped outside my room for many days, and did everything she could. The word paralyzed never left her lips.

After two weeks in ICU and two weeks in the hospital, I was transferred to Dodd Hall in Columbus, Ohio, where I would begin rehabilitation. When I could finally sit upright, my mom wheeled me outside for a picnic. In the distance, we watched a marching band –

my eyes focused on the baton twirler. I thought, "Give me that baton, I can twirl it," but I knew if someone put the baton in my hands, it would slide right through my fingers. I turned to my mom, and I couldn't stop crying.

The words of a friend rang in my head. "You can become bitter, or you can become better." I realized I could lie in bed hopeless, or channel my energy toward therapy and progress. My mom hung signs that said, "Attitude is Everything" all around the rehab unit, and a friend gave me a poster that said, "I can do all things through Christ who gives me strength." It became my life verse and motivational motto.

Walking victoriously through life has nothing to do with legs; it's your attitude, and what's inside your heart.

All my energy became committed to my recovery. I learned to eat with a fork strapped to my hand. I lifted 1/2 pound weights with my wrists and two-pound weights with my arms. My mom helped move my fingers and stretched my legs daily.

I learned to write, dress, even put in contact lenses with barely mobile fingers. Then one day I moved my big toe. A month later, I moved my left leg. Two months later I learned to walk between parallel bars, then progressed to a platform walker. I vowed to myself to walk out of rehab, and only four months after my accident, I took a few unsteady steps out the door on crutches.

Therapy remained a daily routine and I re-enrolled in college. Mom drove me to class, helped me take notes, and typed papers. Two years later, I walked across the stage at the University of Cincinnati on crutches, graduating magna cum laude, with my mom right by my side.

As a surprise thank you to my mom, I wrote a letter to Regis and Kathie Lee (now Regis and Kelly) for their annual "Mom's Dream Come True" show, telling everything my mom has done for me since my accident. They chose my letter out of thousands, had us on their show – a COMPLETE SURPRISE to my mom – and fulfilled her dream by sending our whole Greek family on a cruise to Greece!

I continue to live life every day fully in my wheelchair. My life is filled with meaningful relationships, a great career as well as sports and recreation. With the use of adaptive equipment I race, play wheelchair rugby, snow ski and water ski. I have even completed thirteen marathons! I might be slow, but I finish the course. By not giving up, I hope to truly inspire others.

My role now is as a motivational speaker and author, sharing my secrets for victorious living despite circumstances. Wanting to empower others to overcome their challenges, I founded my own non-profit organization called, "Walking Victorious: Equipping People to Rise Above the Challenges of Life." My goal is to have the opportunity to speak in every state in the US and in various places around the globe. Every day I move closer to that vision as my phone rings and opportunities come my way.

Adversity brings opportunities greater than we can imagine. In 2002, I was crowned Ms. Wheelchair Ohio, and was the second runner-up for Ms. Wheelchair America. Three times I have been awarded Most Valuable Female Athlete for the Ohio Wheelchair Games. These titles allowed me to educate and advocate for people with disabilities. I also had the privilege of being a chaplain for the 2004 Paralympic Games in Athens, Greece.

Honors like this humble me and make me realize that my life can have incredible influence, although the path getting there was very different than I imagined.

Remembering my journey in a wheelchair the day before my accident, I can't help but think that God had a special plan for my life. I would never change it. I have become a better person; I have learned to be thankful, to ask for help when I need it, and I have grown in my faith and in my appreciation for my family. Most importantly, I have used my disability to make a difference in this world, and that brings lasting fulfillment.

Leading an exceptional life is not having exceptional circumstances. It's focusing on others. That is what makes an exceptional life. Walking victoriously through life has nothing to do with legs; it's your attitude, and what's inside your heart.

There is a special plan for your life, too. Don't make excuses; use your life circumstance for a something truly exceptional rather than wishing things were a different way. My wheelchair has given me more rewarding opportunities than my legs ever did. There might be possibilities awaiting you that will be even more fulfilling than before. Create meaning from your pain. Ask yourself, "What can I learn from this? How can I grow? How can I help others?" And then go and make it happen. Your exceptional life begins NOW!

Stacy James
Director of Walking Victorious
Professional Speaker
Dublin, OH
614-889-5785
stacy@walkingvictorious.com
www.walkingvictorious.com

What's Your Story?

CHRISTOPHER YOUNG

LIFE IS a series of stories - some good, some not-so-good. The biggest challenges I have faced have been as a result of the negative stories I created. I used to be an angry, stupid victim.

Oh, I didn't walk around consciously thinking I was angry, stupid, and a victim. It just pervaded my thoughts and expressed itself through my behavior and attitude as a youth and young adult.

The first part of my angry, stupid victim story was created when my stepfather frequently told me that I was stupid between my seventh and twelfth birthdays. Long after his arrest and exit from my life, the "I am stupid" story was my own. I acted stupidly, got into trouble, and chose not to apply myself in school. After all, why study if you are stupid? I lived my story to the fullest.

During my early teens I learned that children who have been physically, sexually, and emotionally abused are called "victims." I liked the idea of someone feeling sorry for me, so I chose to be a victim. If there was an Academy Award for Best Victim, I would have been in the running. The "I am a victim" label fit right in with my "I am stupid" story to become "I am a stupid victim." How do stupid victims act? Like stupid victims.

In high school, I felt so sorry for myself that I became very angry – especially with my mother. This anger grew when I became a foster child. My new and improved story became, "I am an angry, stupid victim."

How do angry, stupid victims act? You guessed it. Not particularly bright, very angry, and much like a victim. I was good at it!

After high school, I took a year off to save for college. School loans and hard work supported me during my first year of college. Interestingly, over the course of that year, the story, "I am stupid" didn't come up. It was replaced by "I must get good grades to get a scholarship and I am paying for it!" As a result, my second year was partially paid by a scholarship that I was awarded. I graduated with a 3.46 GPA. I wasn't stupid after all.

After graduate school, I was 25 and working as a successful angry victim. I wanted to get back what I didn't have as a child and I wanted interest. I drove everyone including my wife and myself crazy. I worked ridiculous long hours, made good money, and was very angry.

At this time, I didn't believe in God and I didn't believe in "foo foo happy talk" thought processes. These were for the weak. I was more interested in making money, being angry, and living a long life.

Then I watched as people I admired and loved began growing older and facing major health challenges. I noticed their changed life perspective after the immediate health challenge had been conquered. It amazed and worried me. I knew that if I wasn't careful, my stress would eventually create similar challenges for me. I asked myself, "Do I have to be 45 and having a heart attack to realize I need to make some changes?"

Thus began a chain of events… With the coming birth of our first child, I was at the height of my anxiety and anger. I was determined to give my daughter the life I didn't have. It was now time to confront my biggest demon, my stepfather, and make him pay. I needed my past completely behind me. I found where he lived and developed a letter to let the small community he lived in know what kind of monster they lived near. Before mailing it, I had to be sure I had the right person so I called him.

Without realizing it at the time, the "I am an angry victim" story had been dealt a death blow.

It was just like the movies…My mind raced as I dialed and then heard the sound of his voice. I was seven years old again and vulnerable. I mustered up what courage I had and told him about the flashbacks, what a monster he was in my life, and how I wished he were dead. He listened patiently and after I was done, he said, "I need to ask for your forgiveness... I have Jesus in my life now."

Remember the Church Lady played by Dana Carvey from Saturday Night Live? I heard the words echo in my head, "How conveeeenient!" That thought was immediately followed-up with an image in my head of a door where the door was open just a crack. I heard a voice say, "Run!" I ran through that door of forgiveness and said, "I forgive you."

I believe these three words have completely changed the direction of my life.

Before this powerful moment in my life, I was consumed with anger and hate. I couldn't go anywhere without feeling negatively – especially back home to North Dakota. After forgiving my stepfather,

I immediately felt better. Over the following days and weeks, I felt profoundly better. Without realizing it at the time, the "I am an angry victim" story had been dealt a death blow.

A few months later, my first child was born and I quit my stressful job to move back to Bismark, North Dakota. I was free to go back and do something that inspired my soul.

Today, my faith is strong and I know I am here on this earth to be a contribution to others on purpose. Every story I put into my head is there because I want it to be. My stories serve a purpose rather than haunt me.

My personal challenge to you is to check your stories and help others with theirs. Are your stories contributing to your life or are they taking away important life energy? How about your loved ones, your co-workers, your friends?

We all need encouragement that will help us reframe our stories.

We are all here in this journey called life for a purpose. I believe what happens to each of us isn't an accident. Everything has purpose. What I choose to do with my story is up to me. My story is now, "I am a contribution and I am making a difference."

Christopher Young
Founder, Difference-Maker, and Inspirational Speaker
The Rainmaker Group
701-319-4150
cyoung@teamrainmaker.com
www.teamrainmaker.com
Blog - www.mastermystories.com

One Snap, Please

CAROL WATSON PhD

I WATCHED in fascination as long, slim brown fingers carefully folded the small sheet of lined paper over and over again. I wasn't certain what my newfound Indian friend was creating, but the smile on his face, the warmth of his large brown eyes, and the ease in which he moved assured me that he knew exactly what he was crafting. The paper folds completed a small square which, when positioned properly on one's fingertips, easily opened into a sunburst. The final touch was a small hole placed in the center of that sunburst. The boy's smile indicated that he'd successfully folded his paper and created something special.

But what he had created was beyond me. I spoke no Telegu, his native language, and he spoke very little English. I could only wonder where the next step of our budding relationship would take us. "One snap please!" were the boy's first words during this encounter and he gleefully lifted what I suddenly realized was a paper camera to his right eye! I posed with my grandest smile as he snapped my picture and then we laughed heartily at the thoughts of our fun afternoon. "One snap please!" was repeated again and again.

For nearly an hour we moved throughout our compound snapping numerous photos of teens at work and play. What a glorious hour it was as we captured the exuberance of daily life in a village in India! We snapped candid shots and staged humorous scenes created with the assistance of willing models. Teens and their adult chaperones both found joy and much needed distraction in our paper camera and impromptu photo shoot before wind and rain forced us to seek shelter in a nearby classroom.

Did I mention that we were in the midst of a cyclone? More than one hundred teens, chaperones, and American volunteers had spent most of the past two days indoors as the torrential rains beat with a powerful hostility and gale force winds destroyed buildings, trees and power lines. I was serving in India with an international teen organization whose mission is to train tomorrow's leaders today. The training phase of our program had barely begun when the deadly cyclone hit. Shortly following the final wave of the cyclone, family members made their way to our training camp to check on the well being of their teens. Some took their teens with them, knowing their help was needed to rebuild homes. Others asked that we continue to care for their children. These caring parents and adult relatives mourned their losses and sought much needed resources to sustain day-to-day life and rebuilding efforts. Entire villages had been washed away and lives had been lost. This was not the first cyclone to hit the area. The teens I was with were well aware of the aftermath this type of storm could produce. Times were tense for everyone involved and yet a simple, paper camera had lightened the burden and provided laughter, just when it was needed the most.

> **So often one is tempted to wait for the perfect moment, the perfect job, the perfect mate, or the perfect opportunity to arrive before experiencing joy.**

Tending to be all too serious most of the time, I'd spent countless hours with other volunteers and group leaders in discussing matters relating to the cyclone - group safety, daily scheduling, program continuation, and potential outcomes of the deadly storm. Disease, lack of medical supplies and food topped our list. Serious matters called for serious prayer and serious action! The responsibility for the teens as well as the continuation of the program weighed heavily on our hearts. Strength, stamina, cooperation, wisdom and God's leading would be vital to our success.

Incredibly, God chose a young teen to lighten my load that afternoon. It was time spent with a newly found Indian friend creating laughter with a paper camera and the simple request, "One snap, please!" that revived my soul and renewed my strength.

I am confident that I have heard the phrase "Find joy in the journey" many times, but I'm not certain that I had ever fully understood or applied those words before. Amazingly, those tumultuous cyclone filled days in India led me to discover this principle that I have applied to my life many times since! So often one is tempted to wait for the perfect moment, the perfect job, the perfect mate, or the perfect opportunity to arrive before experiencing joy. I've learned that the perfect time to experience joy is now, in whatever moment you find yourself. Each of us is on an exceptional walk created just for us by our Heavenly Father. Our entire life is designed to be an exceptional journey. When one learns to embrace each moment, even the darkest ones, the journey is sweetened with an exuberance of wonder and joy.

Carol J. Watson, PhD
Speaker and Author
570-437-2720
cjw141@yahoo.com

Empty Arms

TAMMY ADAMS

*"So much has been given to me; I have no time to
ponder over that which has been denied."*
~ Helen Keller

I LOVE to juggle. I'm not great at it, but I do manage to keep three objects in the air for short periods of time. As for life, I often find myself trying to juggle too many obligations, which is not something I enjoy.

I used to think that my exceptional life would begin when I married and completed the happy picture with children of my own; however, I was never quite sure how well I would juggle the multiple roles of wife, mom and career person.

I married at 38 to a husband who was then 41. We tried right away to have children as the biological clock was ticking louder and louder. It was unsuccessful for three years. Finally, three months after going on 'mood-altering' fertility drugs, my doctor confirmed what I suspected … I was pregnant at the age of 41.

Just two months into this new world of expectant motherhood, my doctor scheduled a genetic counseling appointment. My husband and

I showed up for the next step in this journey, having NO IDEA that this appointment would define the journey. First came the ultrasound, amazing technology that allowed us to see this tiny moving baby. We were sure he or she was waving to us as those arms and legs moved about at an energetic pace. We were on cloud nine as we could see this child we had hoped for, now living and waving. I remember thinking, 'Thank God this baby is alive!'

Your exceptional life can only be embraced if there is room in your life to take hold of it.

The physician came in, took over the testing, and abruptly remarked, "I can already tell this is not going to be a normal pregnancy. I am almost 100% sure this baby will have problems." In a matter of seconds, our long-awaited excitement came to a screeching halt and was replaced by speechless devastation. I remember feeling as if I was suffocating, hardly able to get enough breath to ask the doctor questions.

The drive home with my husband was marked by deafening silence. I fought back tears. Having been a singer all my life, I turned to a familiar place for comfort … music! A favorite CD played Christian songs that broke through the silence. Tears, hurt and pain poured out of me in keeping with the music as God's love began to fill me through the lyrics and message of each song. It was as if God had tailored the order of the songs on that CD to meet the exact needs of my heart.

We finally arrived back home and began calling our closest friends and family members, asking them for prayerful support. God gave me a peace in the midst of my pain, beginning that day while we drove home. He let me know He was fully in control.

Twelve long days later, on a Monday morning, I knew that something was wrong. I followed my intuition and drove to my physician's office, waiting in my car until the office opened. I was escorted to a treatment room where another ultrasound revealed what my heart already suspected. This time, the physician said, "I don't see a heartbeat."

The word miscarriage meant that I must now come to terms with the realization that this baby who waved to me just days earlier, later named Alex, was now a citizen of Heaven. That meant my husband and I would have 'empty arms' this side of Heaven.

I believe that this experience has taught me that our exceptional life is a choice rather than a product of our circumstances. It has reminded me that the things we long for, but cannot have, often serve to help us remember and appreciate who and what we do have in our lives. Our faith, rich life experiences and significant relationships cannot be replaced.

I have been reminded, with Alex as my teacher, that empty arms, while painful at times, create the time and space for God to bring the unexpected into our lives at any moment. Full arms that carry too much work, a never-ending "to-do" list, and endless obligations on our calendar can actually limit us from having room to embrace the best of life.

I have learned that my empty arms give God the divine opportunity to fill my life with so much more than I could ever ask or imagine. If I never experience pregnancy again, I am grateful to have had those three months of expectant motherhood. And I rest in the peace of knowing that one day my arms will be filled in Heaven…as I embrace Alex for the first time.

Meanwhile, my arms are far from empty. My life is full. This unexpected journey has drawn me closer to and into a deeper appreciation of my faith and those who love me ... the two keys to every truly exceptional life. I choose to view my 'empty arms' not as arms that echo loss but as arms that have room for the unexpected to come into my life at any moment. After all, your exceptional life can only be embraced if there is room in your life to take hold of it.

Take it from me. Life is too short, as Helen Keller stated, to sit around contemplating what we wish filled our arms. Go out and embrace the best of life today ... you just may find the truly exceptional comes in unexpected places and fills you with unimaginable joy.

Addendum: Just before Your Exceptional Life Begins Now *went to print, my husband and I learned that our 'empty arms' will not remain empty for long ... we are expecting again, and filled with hope for a new story to emerge.*

Tammy Adams
Physical Therapist Assistant, Vocalist
828-312-1768
dadams692@aol.com

It's Time!

JANICE McMILLIAN

IT'S TIME. These were the words that were spoken to me one Friday evening while arranging the many piles of work on my desk in anticipation of leaving for the weekend. I looked around but realized it was just me in the office, everyone else had departed to start their "Thank God it's Friday" dance. It's time…but time for what?

Had I forgotten so quickly what had transpired just three months earlier. I was ready to say goodbye to a job that seemed to have lost its luster. I got tired of doing the same thing repeatedly day after day without thought to rhyme or reason. I was ready to hand in the resignation and step into that place where uncertainty lived. But, the voice said, no. Was I just imagining things when I heard it? "What do you mean 'no'?" After all, I have a plan. But, my plan was not the perfect plan nor was it the right time.

So, what did I choose to do? I submitted to the voice and laid down my short-sighted agenda to wait for the bigger plan. This meant staying in a place that was literally draining my creativity and my energy.

I obeyed until such time when I would be able to make my departure. But, never would I have imagined it coming so quickly. Only three months since receiving the 'no,' did I receive permission to step into purpose and it happened on a Friday evening at 5:30 p.m. I knew within the depth of my soul that this was for me. The very fiber of my being responded with a resounding YES! I knew that I had just been given permission to do what I was fearfully and wonderfully created to do. The time had arrived.

God, who is "the voice," opened the door for me to experience a whole new level of living. A chapter was about to be written and God was the one with the pen in hand as a ready writer. My role was to simply be obedient and faithful to what He had called me to do.

I believe success needs to be redefined and personalized to our own individual lifestyle rather than simply following what society says it should be.

I've come to realize that the voice of purpose is often compressed deeply because we move about life doing what we must do as opposed to doing what we were created to do. And there is a dramatic difference when you step into the reality that your innate gifts, talents, and abilities can bring fulfillment into your life and into the lives of those whom you impact. Life is a fleeting moment. To continue operating on the assembly line day in and day out, not fully plugged into what gives you passion, deadens you on the inside. Just walk down any downtown street during core business hours and notice the stoic faces of the walking dead going to and from their passionless jobs. Each day a little piece of them is chipped away because they have bought into the notion that they have to do it "this way" in order to succeed. I believe success needs to be redefined and personalized to our own individual lifestyle rather than simply following what society says it should be.

I have been granted an opportunity to use what I am gifted at, and that is writing. God has pointed me through wide open doors to a plethora of assignments and projects that allow me to freely use my gift. I am certainly on a faith walk toward even greater opportunities because my life is in His hands. Each day there is a new adventure to experience and a new unveiling of His dynamic plan for me because I have relinquished the striving and the pursuing that comes along with trying to accomplish things on my own terms.

As a result, my business is a success, not because my bank account is overflowing (although I know as I continue to sow into my purpose, I shall reap) because what I am doing is tied into changing people's lives for the better.

As I have been given the opportunity to tap into what brings me fulfillment, I pray that you will allow your passion and God-given gifts to rise to the surface. Don't be afraid to make a change in your life. There are risks with every decision we make; however, the risks are minimized when we do it God's way. He is more than able to look after and guard over that which He has birthed in us. The question is, do we really trust Him with our life?

I would encourage you to be proactive in the pursuit of your dreams and visions and do something every day to get closer to what makes your heart glad. We only get one chance to come this way, so make it your best life. It's time!

Janice McMillian
President, J. Marie Concepts
jmarie@j-marieconcepts.com
www.j-marieconcepts.com

Wait On God – It's Worth It

LINDA L BUTLER

DO YOU remember the last time you wanted something so bad that you could hardly wait? Perhaps it was a new house, another job, a spouse, or children. What ever it was, you thought about it constantly. You probably even tried to plan just how you could obtain it. So what happened? Did you wait on God or did you go get it yourself? Waiting on God will bring you the very best of what you desire and even more.

I spent nine of the fourteen years that I worked on my first full-time job, working during the day and going to school at night. Although, I knew that the education would payoff later, it was still a challenge to stay focused. Obtaining a higher education was my goal and I had to make many sacrifices to get it. I couldn't buy as many clothes and shoes as I would have liked. I didn't take trips or go on vacations and I couldn't drive a luxury car like some of my friends were doing. I had a nice car, but it wasn't exactly what I wanted…it was what I could afford.

Finally, the day had arrived, I had earned my masters degree and I was graduating. That was definitely one of the best days of my life. It was somewhat unbelievable, going to school had become a way of life for me, but I was looking forward to the free time. Since I had worked so hard to get to this day, I thought that I should reward my self. I should buy the car of my dreams. After all, I was single with no dependents, so why not? Little did I know that the car of my dreams would be so expensive.

I had my sights set on a nice luxury car, such as a Lexus or an Acura. I wanted one with all the bells and whistles - leather seats, sunroof, CD player, etc. After all I deserved it. I could hardly pass by a dealership without stopping to look at one of these cars. With every test drive, I prayed for a miracle, since that's what it was going to take for me to own one of these cars.

It was well worth the wait, God had answered my prayers. It wasn't exactly what I had asked for...it was so MUCH MORE!

Of course, I could have gone out on a limb and purchased a car. It would have been a struggle to keep it and I didn't want to go that route. Besides, I had asked God for a special blessing. I had asked God to bless me with a new luxury car, loaded with options within a specific price range. I knew that I was asking for a miracle and I couldn't wait to see how God would respond.

When I said that I couldn't wait...well, I really couldn't. It seemed like God was taking too long to answer my prayer. I decided that he needed a little help. I visited numerous dealerships, trying to trade my car and I even tried to sell it, but nothing would work out. I remember one time making a "For Sale" sign for my car. I was going to take it to a shopping mall to try to sell it. As I printed the signs, some of the text didn't show up. I thought that there was something wrong with my printer, so I tried it again. It happened again. By now I was beginning to think that God was trying to tell me something. I heeded the warning and threw the signs away, although I couldn't understand why He wouldn't allow me this one thing.

After that incident, I tried a couple of more times to sell my car. No one seemed to be genuinely interested. I had only one person to take it for a test drive. I couldn't understand because it was a very nice car. I had purchased it new, I kept up all the maintenance (with records) and washed it every week. It was in excellent condition. Suddenly the realization came that maybe I shouldn't sell it after all.

A few years later, I paid off my car and I was hopeful again. Only this time, I wasn't very persistent in my search for a luxury car. Something had changed, and although I still wanted the car, I remember my prayer. I had not found a car in the price range that I wanted and I was beginning to think that the opportunity wouldn't ever come my way. I had made this miraculous request and given the results to God. By now my priorities were focused on my career rather than a new car. Although I had recently received a promotion, I was trying to figure out what was next in my life. That internal search meant looking for a new job. I liked the area that I lived in and I wasn't looking to move. I had a cute little apartment and was planning to buy a house. My older sister and her family lived only 5 minutes away and things were going well for me.

One day my younger sister called to give me a message from a company that had been trying to reach me. This was a local company that I had applied to right after graduation and I was told that I didn't have the required experience for the job. I returned the call to find out more about the position. I was immediately scheduled for an interview for a position in Human Resources. After a couple of interviews and a rigorous physical examination, I was offered a job. I went to work for car manufacturer as a Human Resource representative.

You guessed it, my prayer was answered. As part of my benefits, I got to lease a company car and it was under the price point that I was seeking all along. Amazing! I started my new job in June and by end of July, I was driving a brand new car. And yes, it was fully loaded…at last, my long awaited luxury car.   It was well worth the wait, God had answered my prayers. Not only was it what I had asked for, it was so much more. I got a wonderful car and I also got a new job with a great company. God had shown me a very valuable lesson in patience. It had been three years since I made my request and it wasn't until I left the results up to God and changed my focus that things fell into place.

What are you waiting for? Perhaps it's a new job, a new house, a spouse or maybe even a new car? What ever it is be patient, and don't overlook the lessons that you can learn along the way. It will keep you from missing out on what life has to offer. When you least expect it, your time will come and it will be worth the wait.

Linda L Butler
Associate Recognition Professional,
Professional Writer and Author
Greer, South Carolina
LindaButlerSC@aol.com

Leading FROM the Heart

JAMES A VOSSLER

ON SEPTEMBER 13, 1955 a young father sang his own rendition of Jim Reeve's song "Bimbo" live on a local radion station telecast in honor of his newborn son. Thus, my nickname became, has become, and will forever be "Bimbo".   This young father had a plethora of experiences and challenges during his lifetime.   This included fulfilling an obligation to serve his country in WW II where he was captured, tortured, and eventually escaped from a POW camp leading to a Purple Heart decoration.   Julius, my father, left our family when my sister and I were very young. This departure made our family dependent on our grandparents, the welfare system, and our amazing mother, Ellen. She remarried three more times, which enriched our childhood and created many challenging life experiences. As difficult as these experiences were, they served as a springboard that created opportunities for a very productive professional life including coaching, teaching mathematics, and directing educational programs at a large healthcare facility as well as a very well respected university.

Leading FROM the Heart is a synopsis of lessons learned from these personal and professional life experiences.

Most of my childhood was spent playing baseball, basketball, billiards and bowling. In addition to sports, school came easy for me. It became the place to go every day to see great friends and wonderful teachers. At age 16 I met Jim McPherson, teacher and basketball coach, the first of my many mentors. He noticed I had potential and insisted I "conform to reform and perform" as a member of his basketball team. The experience with Coach "Fireball" could be a book in itself. Jim preached, taught, and believed "Being born in America immediately makes you one of the luckiest people in the world because of all the opportunities and advantages…all you have to do is learn to take them!"

Leaders understand that there is a difference between managers and leaders. That is, managers manage things and leaders lead people. That's what Leading from the Heart is all about!

Coach Fireball's impact on young people in my hometown, Williston, North Dakota for over two and one half decades is immeasurable. He was simply outstanding. He is truly a servant leader.

I have been blessed with two daughters, Annie and Maddie, who have grown into fine young women and are becoming great contributors to society. They simply amaze me with their positive attitudes, boundless energy, contagious enthusiasm and constant drive for perfection. The mother of these two girls, Kris, is the greatest mother on the planet. Unfortunately, several years ago we decided we could no longer be married. However before the separation, we agreed our children needed us to lead them as parents not merely befriend them. We believed that we were not raising children but adults and that associations they developed would provide opportunities to influence and be influenced. We become whom we associate with. So instead of asking ourselves "What sort of children do we want?" we asked ourselves "What sort of adults do we want?" It worked. Servant leadership, putting others before ourselves, even in parenting works!

Childhood experiences, living in the chaotic teenage society, competing in athletics, growing professionally and even parenting have helped reinforce the importance of embracing the notions of positive attitude and servant leadership for self fulfillment.

Attitude is a state of feeling or mindset about a person or situation. It is the way we do everything and it is very observable. Attitude is a choice and is more important than money, education, even what other people think or say or do. Attitude comes from within, from the heart. Great leaders have great attitudes. Leaders understand that there is a difference between managers and leaders. That is, *managers manage things and leaders lead people.* There is a difference. Effective leaders have common traits: They are competent, they have values and they share their God given gifts with others in abundant amounts. That is, they extend themselves as servant leaders to everyone, especially to those in need. They simply help other people...constantly. They also understand the importance of mission statements, not only in organizations but also in their personal lives. They believe that mission statements serve as a guide for life's choices. Mission statements tell you what to do when "You don't know what to do."

There is so much for all of us to learn and so many different ways for us to learn. Life experiences have been the greatest learning tool for me. I would like to share lessons learned.

- ▸ Feelings are neither good nor bad, just feelings. Never apologize for your feelings.
- ▸ We should expect life to be difficult. That doesn't mean life can't be good...just expect relationships, school, work, parenting and all that to be challenging. Then you won't be disappointed and you'll be better prepared.
- ▸ Difficult times reveal your character. Never compromise your character.

- Love yourself, without that, you'll never be able to share love with others.
- Know the difference between caring for and taking care of. There is a difference. Caring for is an act of love while taking care of can be "codependency."
- Forgiveness is second only to prayer. Learn to forgive.
- Share your talent and wealth with others. You can experience great joy from serving mankind.
- You have seven seconds to make an impact on someone you meet for the first time. Make a good first impression.
- Woody Allen is right, 70% of success is just showing up. Be where you say you're going to be and do what you say you're going to do.
- Own a pet. It allows you to understand God's work from a different perspective.
- Life is full choices. Take responsibility for the ones you make and learn from mistakes. If you make the same mistake over and over again, get help.
- Beware of victims and control freaks. Victims don't take enough responsibility for their situation and control freaks take too much. Both can be horrible influences.
- Perfection is something to strive for. Think in terms of PERFECT.
- Know that winning and losing can be good things. No one wins all the time. Great lessons can be learned from losing.
- Understand what is in your own heart so you can better understand what is in the hearts of others.
- Happiness is a personal choice, unfortunately, so is misery. Choose to be happy.
- Attitude is important and behavior reflects it. Behave well.
- Love life one day at a time. It is said yesterday is the past, tomorrow is the future and today is a gift…that's why they call it the "present."

- Life is a journey, don't look back. That is why the windshield on your car is approximately fifty times as large in area as the rearview mirror. Don't ignore the past just don't dwell on it. Be forward looking and forward thinking.
- Have class. If you don't have class, it doesn't matter what else you do have no one will notice anyway. And if you have class you really don't need anything else.

Finally, and above all else, our purpose is to serve God. Discover your gifts and learn how to share them with your loved ones and all of mankind.

James A. Vossler
Upward Mobility Specialist
The Rainmaker Group
jim@teamrainmaker.com
www.teamrainmaker.com

The Sound of a Shifting Life

SHARON DESJARLAIS

"Don't close your eyes. This is your life.
Are you who you want to be?"
From *This Is Your Life* by Switchfoot

AS A MOTHER, the most devastating thing you can imagine is losing a child.

From the moment I gave birth to my daughter Devin, I was gripped with insecurity and fear. Would I be a good mom? Could I protect her from strangers? Would I keep her safe and well fed?

I was young, of course, and slowly became more confident in my parenting skills. A brown-eyed beauty, Devin was growing up nicely. She was bright and bubbly and fun.

Then one day about eight years ago, our lives unexpectedly shifted and in a very real sense, my daughter died.

It began on Christmas Eve when Devin was eight years old. She and her dad had just spent a few days baking cookies for our neighbors in keeping with their annual holiday tradition.

I stepped into a home filled with the sweet, buttery aroma of shortbread cookies. But what grabbed my attention were the odd yelping sounds. They were coming from Devin.

At that point we had been seeing the signs of something strange for several weeks. Normally an outgoing child, Devin had become confused and withdrawn. She had taken to scrunching her nose and squinting her eyes. And she'd started mumbling under her breath, as if whispering to someone who wasn't there in a language we couldn't understand.

Frankly, we were less worried than annoyed. We assumed her unusual facial and vocal tics were some kind of habit she had picked up. Sadly, we assumed wrong.

A few days after Christmas I took Devin for a check-up. In the treatment room, she continued to yelp and blurt out unintelligible sounds. The doctor examined her with a stunned look on his face, then turned to me and made his pronouncement.

"Tourette's Syndrome," he said, with a tight, rigid smile. Yet his eyes looked sad.

My body froze. I struggled to breathe. All I could recall about Tourette's Syndrome was something I had seen on television. A man with Tourette's had been on trial. His tics made a spectacle out of him. His body jerked with raggedy spasms, and his testimony was riddled with curse words he couldn't control.

Now this doctor was telling me that Devin – my delightful little girl– had this strange, inexplicable affliction.

The diagnosis was devastating. My husband, a therapist who often works with terminally ill children, was shocked but able to put it into perspective. "I guess there are worse things," he said. "At least she isn't dying."

If that was true, then why did I feel like she had? For weeks I cried myself to sleep every night. Each morning was like waking up to the nightmare all over again.

That's when it hit me. I *was* mourning the death of my daughter – or at least the idea of who I thought she would be.

In *The 7 Habits of Highly Effective People*, author Stephen R. Covey says each of us is guided by two categories of maps stored in our heads: maps of the way things are, and maps of the way we think things should be.

We interpret everything we experience through these mental maps, he says. "We seldom question their accuracy; we're usually even unaware that we have them. We simply assume that the way we see things is the way they really are or the way they should be."

With that single decision, Devin's world began to unfold around her. "People who stayed away from me because I was so angry about having Tourette's started to become my friends," she says.

There are times, he adds, that we suddenly become enlightened and our perception changes. These "paradigm shifts" allow us to see things in a new light. But sometimes that shift can be painful – especially when it signals the death of a dream.

I realized then that I had spent years carefully constructing an image of Devin in my mind. I imagined her breezing through life, attracting friends and being the center of attention for all the right reasons.

Unfortunately, the daughter I'd dreamed up had become more real to me than who she actually was. And when I found out she was someone different, the image I held of her inside of me died.

That's when I was privileged to witness Devin's birth for the second time in my life. I watched as she slowly became the person she'd always been. Sweet, messy, insightful, aggravating, courageous – and the true potential for all she has since become.

Devin taught me the meaning of strength as I watched her deal with years of humiliation. Like the time she overheard a classmate asking her teacher if they could lock her away in a soundproof box. Or when she was at the movies and couldn't control her cursing. Or when she marched up to the school stage to accept an award, violently shaking her head every step of the way.

Devin taught me the meaning of authenticity, character and choice. She was only thirteen years old when she decided she no longer wanted to be a victim of her circumstances.

"I didn't want to be afraid anymore," she says. "And I was tired of not having any friends. So I made it a point to be different, to reach out to other people."

With that single decision, Devin's world began to unfold around her. "People who stayed away from me because I was so angry about having Tourette's started to become my friends," she says. "I allowed myself to come out of my shell and become the happy, easygoing person I was inside before I was diagnosed."

Today Devin is a kind and compassionate sixteen year old girl. Blessedly, her tics faded away soon after she started high school. Yet the results of her choices remain. She has a huge group of friends who love her for her sensitivity and quirky sense of humor. "I've become my true self," Devin says.

Now, as a life purpose and career coach, I specialize in helping other women and teenage girls discover the gifts inside of them. With Devin as my inspiration, I guide them to shift into their true natures as the creative, empowered individuals they are so they can work with joy every day.

After all, I tell them, this is YOUR life. No matter what struggles you're faced with, you still get to decide who you want to be.

Sharon Desjarlais
Your True-Calling Coach™
Certified Life Purpose and Career Coaching
Discover your life purpose and work with joy
www.yourtruecallingcoach.com
sharon@yourtruecallingcoach.com

Who Wants to Talk to a Drunk?

BOB FLETCHER

*"In opening our arms to another, we put out a welcome sign
that implies we have made room for them inside ourselves…
For that reason, to the degree we open our arms, we are changed."*
~ Dan Allender

I MUST begin by turning back the clock to December 1967. I had taken a job driving a truck for my brother in law, hauling produce from Florida. As most truckers, I had developed a habit of making the same stops on a regular basis. One of those stops occurred in South Georgia along US 301 before Interstate 95 was built.

I usually stopped at the Jerome Truck Stop late at night and placed my usual order for pie and trucker's coffee. On this particular night, I stopped and joined only a couple of other people in the diner … the usual waitress and a local drunk. I placed my order. As it was delivered, I noticed the local guy looking around at me as he moved out of his booth by the window. The last thing I wanted at 2:00 a.m. was to have a drunk interrupt my break. I dropped my head to avoid making eye contact; however, he came directly to me and stopped beside my booth. I looked up and spoke. With a sad expression, he asked if he could talk with me. Reluctantly, I said yes. After all, who wants to talk to a drunk?

He took a seat and began by noting that he had seen me before. Then he said something that surprised me ... "You are different than most." "How is that?," I asked curiously. He went on to explain that he had taken note of the fact that I always prayed over my food. I thanked him for noticing.

He began to tell me that he was in a terrible set of circumstances and wanted me to pray for him. I then asked him if he knew Jesus Christ. He said, "No, I don't." I explained to him that the Bible tells us that if we have Christ in our hearts, no problem is too big for God to handle. I went on to explain that God has equal love and acceptance of each of us, despite our circumstances. He seemed to doubt that this could be true of him.

He asked, "Do you really think he would accept me the way I am?" I assured him that the answer was yes. Tears began to stream down his face. He asked if I would pray for God to forgive and accept him. I agreed and suggested we go to my truck for privacy. His walk to the truck had the sway of alcohol. Once in the truck, he explained that his wife had just given up on him, taking their children to live with another man. Her new home was just down the street in a trailer, near where his broken family had called home.

He opened his heart that night, praying for freedom from alcoholism and asking God to accept him into His Kingdom. I had never seen someone more relieved or grateful. He climbed from my truck and walked straight back into the diner ... the kind of straight that a sober man walks. I drove onto Florida to complete my route that Tuesday night. I usually made two trips each week, but the next day, I was late getting loaded. This caused me to be late for my typical stop at the Jerome truck stop ... I simply didn't have time to stop.

Think about it … opening your arms to another could create a breakthrough that impacts a life beyond your wildest imagination and at just the right time!

The following Sunday, I headed out on schedule, arriving like clockwork in Jerome at 2:00 a.m.. There were a few new faces, but I didn't see James. The usual waitress came to take my order and I asked if she had seen our friend James. She looked at me with shock and said, "Haven't you heard?" She went on to tell me that last week after I had left, James came back into the diner more excited and hopeful than she had ever seen him. He had told the diner staff that he was going to set his life straight and win back his wife and family. The waitress went on to tell me that James left the diner that night with the intention of going to find his wife. He had approached the door of the trailer she was sharing with her new boyfriend … he knocked. The man came to the door armed with a shotgun, shooting James through the door and striking him in the face. He died instantly.

"They buried him Friday," she said. My eyes filled with tears and my heart sank. Then it occurred to me that he had been less than six hours away from dying without Christ in his life, thereby dying without eternal hope, when he and I talked and prayed together less than a week earlier. I have lived with the guilt of having almost turned him away from my booth that night, being too tired to bother with a drunk.

I now know in my heart that when I cross to the other side, I will see James waiting to welcome me. What an exceptional moment that will be!

When that person approaches you at the most un-opportune time for advice or support, what will your response be? Think about it … opening your arms to another could create a breakthrough that impacts a life beyond your wildest imagination and at just the right time!

Bob Fletcher
President, Innovative Leadership Solutions
828-963-0104
bob1@triad.rr.com

Me First

BOB EALING

I GREW up in a small, Midwest town, the youngest of four children and, according to my brother and sisters, the one who was spoiled rotten. From my earliest memories, I loved anything to do with sports. The truth of the matter . . . my world was all about ME – what I could do, what I could achieve, and how I could achieve it. Significant success in sports brought me attention, accolades and awards, all contributing to "the world of ME."

I met my wife, Chris, in 1966 and was drafted into the Army six months after our marriage in 1968. The Army shipped me overseas two weeks before our first anniversary and I returned two weeks after our second. It was during this period that the ME in my life really took over. I lived much of that time overseas like I was single, certainly not as a man committed to his wife. I am not sure you have experienced these temptations in your life, but I can assure you that these times of unfaithfulness and selfishness left me with a pit in my stomach. I knew my behavior was wrong but I was too proud and macho to admit it to myself. After all, life was all about ME.

When I returned home, it was like starting over with Chris. We were married strangers for awhile, but gradually settled into a life of adventure with graduate school, the births of two sons, cross-country moves, and a succession of jobs in corporate America. There remained, however, an underlying emptiness in my life and I felt neither happy nor fulfilled.

Just where did this selfish, "ME first", life leave me? Short tempered and angry with Chris and our sons, uncharacteristically rough with our pet dog, physically ill for seemingly unexplainable reasons, sad and empty inside, missing the joy and happiness that are otherwise a part of who I am, and morally distraught. When you know better and still make wrong, willful decisions, it can wreck your life. That is precisely what it was doing to me.

> **I can't imagine what or who I would have become if I hadn't come face-to-face with God at that point in my life.**

One day, in the midst of this unhappiness, Chris said something to me that resonated deeply and had both a profound and lasting impact. She said, "I don't know what you are going to decide about your life and our marriage but, whatever it is, it's going to be between you and God. You're the one who has to live with what you decide. This is no longer a Bob-and-Chris issue, it's a Bob-and-God issue." That statement from my wife probably saved our marriage and my life.

I can't imagine what or who I would have become if I hadn't come face-to-face with God at that point in my life. It was then that I renewed my commitment and said "yes" to God. You see, I had given my life to Him when I was thirteen, but I had never really stopped living like a spoiled child. Now I was ready to change! This renewed commitment brought me a freedom beyond description and empowered me to begin making changes.

When I examined my relationship with our boys, especially our oldest son, who was ten at the time, it was clear that I had work to do. As I said earlier, one of the results of living my selfish life was an undefined anger that frequently manifested itself in me being short-tempered. While I never hit my kids or screamed at them, my tone of voice and body language sent unmistakably negative messages.

One day I asked Ryan, our oldest son, to sit and talk with me. Actually, as I recall, I did most of the talking. I told him I didn't expect him to respond but that I hoped what I was going to say would be something he would remember forever. I needed my son to know that I was speaking to him from the bottom of my heart and the depths of my soul. I began by apologizing for all the times I had been short-tempered and angry and physical without cause, explaining that he was in no way responsible for my behavior. I asked his forgiveness for running up and down the sidelines at his soccer games, yelling at him and telling him what to do. To this day, I have an indelible memory of my son who looked straight at me during one of those games with an expression on his face that said, "I wish you would just go away." At that moment, I was alone on my island of selfishness and it was truly a time of personal desperation. I cannot tell you how liberating it was to face my son and ask his forgiveness for my past behavior.

During those years of bad decisions and self-focused living, I was spending long hours working. I spent more time and shared more intimately with those with whom I worked than I did with my family. Often, I would come home with the latest self-help book and hand it to my wife. Here I was, telling Chris she should read this book if she wanted to be happier, oblivious to the fact that I was the one who needed changing. When I finally began to allow God to guide my life, I realized that Chris didn't need 'fixing.' She just wanted to be loved and cherished by me.

Now, make no mistake about it, I still find myself occasionally perched on my throne of self-indulgence. It's at these times that God nudges me with a reminder to climb down and continue living by serving and loving others. What a blessing – an awakening – that enabled me to fully embrace a life that has become truly exceptional.

Bob Ealing
Boise, Idaho
208-484-2201
bobealing@movetotheedge.com
www.movetotheedge.com

Running the Race of Life

LISA M HARPER

LIFE IS like a race, and not just any race. Life is like a marathon. It has its times of exhilaration and its times of exhaustion...moments of triumph and those of sheer pain. Yet, when we cross that finish line and all is said and done, the determination in the face of daunting odds is worth it all. I know this from personal experience.

I have had the joy of running six marathons in my lifetime. Two were in 1985, and four have been since 2002. During that seventeen year break, I became a pastor's wife, taught gymnastics and school, earned a Masters Degree, tutored and home schooled, and played the piano or sang at church every week for over a decade. In the midst of all that, I have been pregnant nine times, enduring five disheartening miscarriages.

For me, these miscarriages were a thorn in my side. Yet, I always remembered this wise saying, "Even though the sky is cloudy and gray, the sun is always shining." Think about that! Some situations seem so hopeless, yet with God, truly all things are possible. Though life has dealt me some lemons, God created lemonade when he gave me four delightful children and a supportive husband.

That year I was joined by over seventy-five people who ran various distances for causes beyond themselves. As a group, we concluded that life is not all about us.

It was after these childbearing years that I decided to run a marathon again in my hometown of Detroit, Michigan. After all that I had been through, I never thought I would do THAT again. Twenty-six miles is not like your average cakewalk! Because I wanted to truly make an impact for good, in 2003, I started Marathon Mission, a non-profit faith and community-based charity for walkers and runners.

In 2004, our Marathon Mission became a much more significant charity. Its purpose is to allow walkers and runners to raise financial support for the plethora of outstanding missionaries and charitable workers, both in the United States and around the world, who daily lay down their lives for the less fortunate. That year I was joined by over seventy-five people who ran various distances for causes greater than themselves. As a group, we concluded that life is not all about *us*. It is all about GOD and giving others a hand up.

What I have learned from these last few Detroit Free Press Marathons has been truly amazing. Once I saw a blind man crossing over the Ambassador Bridge into Canada…buddy, cane and all. I though to myself, "If he can endure such hardships with determination and gratitude, so can I." My previous challenges in life seemed to pale in comparison to his. This caused me to give thanks to God with a grateful heart.

Then there were the lessons of preparation and training. Most good things in life take a great deal of discipline, commitment, perseverance, hope, and a willingness to take big risks. For marathon runners, it is crucial that we log those miles months ahead of time and that we drink a lot of liquids. In the same way, while the mundane events in life may not be all that exciting, we can take courage that as we do the right things and sow good seeds, healthy fruit will grow and remain. Just as runners need water, our souls, too, need those daily times of refreshing in God's presence. As I set my heart and mind on things above, life is full of so much more purpose.

What is your purpose in life? What drives you to seek the exceptional life you long for? I experience immeasurable satisfaction when I use my strength to make an eternal impact in the lives of others. My wise mother used to always tell me, "Honey, when you are feeling down, go DO something for someone else." Try it. You will never be the same.

During the last six miles of one of my recent marathons, I remember speaking (almost yelling) words of encouragement to all who would listen. "You're looking great…You should be proud of yourself…Way to go…Keep your head up… There's joy in the journey…You are almost home." In this marathon of life, we all need those encouraging words, don't we? Why is it that we usually wait until people are dead to tell them how much we love and appreciate them? Don't wait any longer, friend.

Perhaps you have felt like you are running this race of life all alone. You are saying, "No one knows the trouble I've seen." However, God knows your struggles. He wants to fill each one of us with new strength and tenacity of purpose. Hebrews 12:1 and 2 reminds us, "Therefore, since we are surrounded by such a great cloud of witnesses… let us run with perseverance the race marked out for us." There truly is a host in heaven cheering us on!

So be of good cheer! The long miles and steep hills of life develop our character. Gold is not gold until it goes through the fire! Learn from life's lessons. Live to give. Life is like a race. Make every mile exceptional!

Lisa M Harper
Director, Marathon Mission
734-397-0937
harpersrun86@wowway.com
www.marathonmission.net

I Know Jack!

JACKIE GEROSIN

WHEN I thought about writing this story, the first thing I thought was "There is really nothing about my life that is any different from the next person." After all, everybody deals with adversity, pain, grief, heartbreak, and we all have to cope with things that are out of our control.

From the time I was a little girl, the child of an alcoholic and drug addict, I thought life just "happened." My life was merely focused on survival. I was always afraid to hope for things or to dream because pain and disappointment were all I knew as a child. Consequently, I learned to live my life in a controlled, safe, conservative way. I experienced a painful dose of reality when I discovered how very little control I actually had over my life.

It began with the birth of our much awaited son, Jack. Like most parents, we were thrilled and excited. The anticipation soon turned to numbing shock and heartbreak. At four months of age, Jack had seizures, developed infantile cataracts and had his first surgery. Hospitalizations, doctors, therapists and vague diagnoses, coupled with his slow development and uncontrolled behaviors, soon consumed our lives.

We took him to physical therapists, speech therapists, surgeons, clinics and specialists of every kind. We felt certain that with today's technology, someone or something could help our baby boy and give us some answers. Hearing words such as, "autism," "brain disorder," and "mental retardation" felt like a hot knife piercing my chest. It always seemed like these things happened to other people – not us! For a young, married couple who always needed to feel "safe" and "normal," our lives were completely out of control. The stress took a toll on our emotional and physical health, as well as our marriage. We kept coming together and leaning on one another until the burdens became too heavy for either of us to bear. We separated, and later divorced after Jack's fifth birthday.

The fear that penetrated me was paralyzing. How was I going to do this alone? How was I going to financially and emotionally survive while taking care of two children? My seven-year-old daughter was raising herself, as Jack required around-the-clock care. During this chaotic time, my stepfather, a man I adored, passed away and Jack was once again hospitalized for constant seizures.

While my son was in the hospital I received the news that he had been accepted to live in a group home for children with developmental disabilities. From my perspective, this was a mixed blessing. On one hand, I knew it would be a wonderful environment for Jack. He would have the appropriate resources on hand at any given time to assist him with all of his special challenges. But how could I turn my child over to someone else? What did that say about me as a mother? And how much loss could one person endure? The rage I felt toward God, my ex-husband, my family, and any woman with a healthy child, is difficult to describe.

Fear, isolation and depression eventually shifted into grief and mourning. I began to realize that I was grieving the "loss" of my son...the child I had dreamed of. I was mourning the child I longed for him to become, but God clearly had another plan.

There is a verse in the Bible that says "God works all things together for the good of those who love Him." (Romans 8:28) I used to think this passage meant life should be "rosy." It is now my belief that we live in a hard place, and that we are here to learn. The greatest lesson I've learned is that we can experience adversity and not just survive...but thrive! God never promised that our lives here would be free of pain. My life certainly has not been a graceful path to finding peace. Yet I realize that through God, peace and contentment can be achieved in the midst of chaos. Healing comes not when we avoid confronting loss, but when we finally decide to respond to it.

Healing comes not when we avoid confronting loss, but when we finally decide to respond to it.

Now, when I look at my son, I don't see a broken, sick child. I see an amazing little soul whom God entrusted to me. He has affected more people in his short time on this planet than most people will in a lifetime. I am so grateful to know Jack. He has certainly been one of my greatest teachers. He has taught me that there can be purpose through pain, and meaning in suffering, and value in every life.

It is my hope that Jack's story will encourage you to imagine the possibilities and to acknowledge the opportunities that may be right in front of you. I think it is God who stirs in us the desire to do something great with our lives. My prayer for you is that you Live Your Exceptional Life, Now.

Jackie Gerosin
Stonebrook Mortgage, Senior Loan Officer
Mom of Two
Boise, Idaho
jgerosin@stonebrookcorp.com

The Power of Pink

LORIE GARLAND

RAISED A southern girl, my approach to life has always been somewhat laid back. The universal definition of laid back has evolved by the experiences I have had, and continue to have throughout my endeavors. These experiences have been a tremendous transition in my life and constantly remind me that I was placed on this earth for a purpose, as each of us has been. Although my thought processes and priorities are constantly changing, I often find myself reflecting back to my childhood. As I seek to find my purpose and reflect on my life, I continually recognize new traits and ambitions that are present within me. With this challenge of observation have come many realizations that not only validate my roots but make me proud of my "southern ways." I am eager to instill those traditions in my children's world so that they may also discover their life purpose. I am convinced that my purpose lies in the hands of those lives that I impact.

> *"Service to others is the rent I pay for my room on earth."*
> ~ Muhammad Ali

I am a "girly-girl." I enjoy dressing nice, having freshly manicured nails, polished toes and trendy hairstyles. My husband describes me best as "Vogue in appearance, with a southern drawl and a spunky personality." My profession is somewhat of a mystery to others, however

I am positive it is all a part of my unique purpose. I work for the Chamber of Commerce in my hometown of Hickory, North Carolina. It is my job to improve the quality of lives and the community as a whole. Interaction in the community is imperative to my work in Catawba County and perhaps what I enjoy the most. I am active within several non-profit organizations that make an impact on the citizens right where we live and work. One such organization is the Foothills Antique Power Association. This group has 180 members whose motto is, "Preserving our past for their future." Members are predominately men who preserve and restore anything power driven. My participation in this organization has been a tremendous learning experience, and a stepping stone toward my life long purpose. I became involved with this club merely as a supporting wife who had an interest and passion for something that I knew little about, antique tractors.

This was a step out of my world of high heels and cute purses to find that sometimes the grass is greener on the other side.

"Change is the only thing that offers new opportunity."
~ Ross Shafer

Keeping with southern tradition, quiet time is important. These moments are spent with my husband, Bryant on our front porch swing, as we would sit and discuss our day. We share a passion…tractor pulling. This is a growing sport across the nation in which you take an antique tractor and challenge others on the strength and ability to pull a sled as you move down the track. I had been attending tractor pulls for years but merely as a spectator. Now, I decided that I wanted to compete. My husband encouraged me to follow my enthusiasm for this great sport. That night on the front porch, we talked about my tractor. We had a vision, and it was a beautiful one. I told Bryant, "If I am going to Tractor Pull, the tractor has to be pretty." The vision was for an old tractor restored back to her original, perfect condition, with one stipulation, she had to be pink. Obviously, pink is my favorite color, however our reasoning was to use the color for recognition and marketing. Pink Power would be her name and she would be a lot like myself, "Vogue in appearance, with a southern drawl and a spunky personality."

Bryant supported my vision and was as excited as I. We never strayed from that vision. Keep in mind, in the world of tractor pulling, these men are passionate about restoring these tractors back to their original beauty. My passion was a little different than those men. I wanted to pull a beautiful powerhouse that not only dominated in appearance and strength but also made other women share my passion. I wanted to get others involved in the sport and to be able to do so with pride and feel no intimidation. As our talks about Pink Power became more frequent and detailed, my expectations grew.

One weekend at a Pull, a friend and fellow member, Jamie, asked if I would like to pull his tractor. At that point, I had never driven his Allis Chalmers tractor which was scheduled to pull in competition very shortly. My excitement outweighed my fear and after a little instruction, I was ready for my first run down the track. Although I had watched and learned from my peers, I was feeling anxious as I backed the tractor up to the sled. As I began to pull, the front tires rose off the ground. I increased my speed and was already halfway down the track. The adrenaline was apparent by the smile on my face. I won second place that day, but most importantly, I found the tractor that would be Pink Power. *I guess you could say we connected.* There was a lot of work to be done in a short amount of time. Our club's Annual Show and Pull was only three weeks away, and I wanted to debut Pink Power there.

With much help, my vision was suddenly a reality. She was absolutely perfect. Pink Power was bubble gum pink with a pearlized reflection that was glass-like in appearance. She had metallic silver flames outlined in black that stretched along the sides, each curved just enough to be feminine. The battery box showed off her name and her seat cover was black and white. The weight brackets were a shiny black and there was a touch of chrome peeking from beneath the hood. On the back rest, was my name written in signature script. I felt as if I had just given birth for the third time, but I was feeling no pain.

We debuted Pink Power that weekend. She received a lot of attention and I gained a lot of respect not only from within the club but within myself. I had taken a year long vision and with help and guidance created a purpose, a passion, and a fresh perspective. This was a step out of my world of high heels and cute purses to find that grass sometimes is greener on the other side. My eagerness and vision outweighed my fears and intimidations and for that I am so thankful.

I look back and think of my life before Pink Power and can't imaging turning back. She has truly improved my life, my marriage and my purpose. She continues to motivate and inspire those that witness her beauty and strength. We compete almost every weekend now and Pink Power continues to make me proud. She is a powerhouse and scores first and second place in most of our competitions. Bryant and I are still enjoying our evening chat sessions on the front porch swings and are now plotting "Pink Power Two." I am still learning, and once in a while I have feelings of intimidation when my competitors are on larger tractors. These feelings disappear as I feel the front wheels rise during a pull. That is just her way of reminding me of my purpose. OH! THE POWER OF PINK.

Special thanks to Bryant for stepping out of the box with me, allowing me to love you, and most importantly, for painting that tractor pink. Thanks to Jamie and Toby for being my friends, my competitors, and for painting that tractor pink.

Lorie Garland
Catawba County Chamber of Commerce
1138 15th Street NE
Hickory, NC 28601
828-310-0488
pinkpower@charter.net
www.pinkpowerpulling.com

The Angels Around Us

DIANNE HOUGH

I HAVE wanted to tell this story for quite some time. It is so special, so truly unique and maybe even miraculous that I have long felt I simply would not be able to do it justice. But it is my story, it happened to (actually I feel for) me, so I'll trust the same Angels that helped me be a participant nearly six years ago will now help me convey the magic of it all. Extraordinary things happen for each of us everyday. We should be open to the possibilities and then our eyes – and hearts – can bear witness to truly incredible events.

My Angels aren't billowy puffs of fog. I don't see them as an image but I do recognize them . . . now. They're inspirations, emotions, positive energy that moves me to take action. And, I'm grateful to get caught up in the energies. This story ends with me walking up to a "perfect" stranger and saying, "You're his mom aren't you?" She replied with her own question, "How did you know?" At that very moment I could tell she already knew the truth as I said, "Your son brought me here." He had died four days before our meeting. . .

My first "sign" was when I had an unusual desire to get to the first scrimmage for my hometown football team, the Boise State Broncos, that year. It was the middle of August 1999. After all I was a cheerleader for that football team some years ago! That gives me a connection, right?

Right! My husband, Bob, and I were big fans. He used to be the President of the Alumni Association back in the years when Boise State played on green turf. How things have changed! That turf is now a vivid blue (Boise State University actually has blue Astroturf in their stadium!) which has helped the Broncos be selected for bowl games and ESPN appearances in recent years. So, when the inspiration came for me to go to the scrimmage I wasn't surprised, though it had been maybe 20 years since we had been to this particular event. Going to an actual game was common. But for us, this scrimmage was a thing of the past. I was very busy with my real estate career and was often too scheduled to take time out for social events, let alone a football scrimmage. But, this nagging drive told me to get to this particular scrimmage. I searched for the details – I really wanted to be there, for some reason.

Being a high producing realtor in Boise, Idaho, requires some pretty long hours. I would just have to stop working a little early – AND GO . . . which I did not do. We were only –oh– an hour late when we entered the stadium. My husband is such a patient man. He'll do anything to make it to a football game, even wait for me. As we walked into that giant arena, I could feel the sadness. Something wasn't right. The sizeable crowd had all but vanished. The stage was set, the stadium lights shown strikingly bright against the nightfall, but there was no game. Only a heavy, rather ominous feeling energy lingered. I said to Bob in a near panic, "We've got to get home and find out what happened here tonight."

And, there it was all over the television. A new, potentially outstanding young player had been injured, maybe seriously. They would know more tomorrow. I knew then. At the very least, I knew who had pushed me to get to the game, even though I didn't KNOW him. Paul Reyna, was his name. He was a freshman linebacker from California who had yet to play in a college football game. After all, this was just a scrimmage. It was just for fun but it set the stage for an outstanding season for my team. On and off the field, Paul was a part of that success.

As Paul lay in a coma for the next five days the stories of how he chose Boise State came out in the media. He had witnessed a cross in the sky on his first visit to the campus and considered that to be his sign to come to Boise. Boise State had won his heart – and now, in a most unexpected way – Paul was winning Boise's heart. The community instantly embraced this young man and rallied to his cause. The Angels were all about us – sharing love, sharing tears, sharing compassion for his family who sent their son to Idaho to fulfill his dreams. In the week that followed the scrimmage, Paul made his everlasting effect on this community – maybe more so than if he had completed four fabulous years of Bronco football. And when he died, a whole town mourned. It was impressive, it was unifying and spiritual. Like so many others, I was drawn into this powerful drama. I read every article and watched for the news briefs on television totally captivated and inspired. I wondered if I was supposed to go to his services – but that wasn't quite right. So I simply stayed tuned – hoping I'd recognize my role whatever it might be.

Sometimes I wonder if our Angels get frustrated with us as we fail to recognize our greater mission. But we're caught in the throws of living itself. All the distractions . . . like make a living, do a good job, make a difference – blah, blah, blah. It's a wonder we ever calm ourselves enough to "see the signs" or "trust unconditionally" – but if you CAN get yourself there – it is so worth it!

I was starting to feel that I missed the boat with this one. Something had me focusing so much on this event – this young man's life – but it was now over. His family had come to town and we had done what we could do as a community to help them say goodbye to Paul. It seemed to be the end of a chapter, but my Angels were still with me. Then, late

We should be open to the possibilities and then our eyes – and hearts – can bear witness to truly incredible events.

Saturday night – it was 12:30 – Bob was giving up on the television and headed to bed. I was feeling too restless for sleep. I needed to GO SOMEWHERE. Then it came to me. I needed to go to Table Rock . . .the place where Boise has a huge lighted cross overlooking the city. From my back door to the top of that hill is a one hour hike and I wanted to go, rather, I needed to go. I turned to our two house guests and said "You want to join me?" They were game to drive, not hike – so we loaded up Kodiak, our Alaskan Malamute and headed up the hill. It's really fun to share this special place with people new to Boise.

As we got out of our SUV on that flat topped foothill adorned with a huge beaming cross, a warm, comforting breeze welcomed us. Maybe it is only safe for such late night adventures in a place like Boise. Maybe the cross yields some protection within its rays of light. Regardless, there is peaceful calm atop that hill. As we approached, the gentle breeze instantly picked up to a strong, playful wind. Kodiak started dancing around on his leash - he didn't know what to do with this exhilarating energy. The whole feeling was joyful and uplifting. As we came closer to the massive quarry rock bench near the edge of the rim rock I could see a few others were also enjoying the night. At that moment, I knew why I had come to this perfect place at this perfect hour. So, with my Angels in tow, I walked up to her and said, "You're Paul's mom aren't you?" She lifted her eyes with a slight sense of relief and said, "Yes." What a glorious moment for us both! We didn't have to try to talk – we just talked. It was obvious to us both that Paul had staged this meeting. She was leaving early in the morning and just wanted to touch him somehow. The very cross that beckoned Paul to Boise was now giving them a venue for their final goodbye. My role was simply to be there for him – and I was! Paul just needed my help, mother to mother and maybe even a bit of the old cheerleader for himself. I was privileged to be there – to share their moment. I'll always be grateful to those Angels (who really are around us everyday) for helping us slow our hectic lives long enough to recognize such extraordinary gifts within our reach. What a rich evening it was, beautifully orchestrated by the Angels themselves!

Dianne Hough, REALTOR®, ABR
Group One, Inc.
Boise, Idaho
dhough@group-one.com

You Just Never Know

JULIE DAY

THE EARLIEST memories that I have in life are that of my childhood home. The place where I lived was anything but typical. It was a small house nestled beside the Davis Packing Company, which was a slaughterhouse in the 1940's. It was located in Garden City, a not so wealthy section of Boise, Idaho. It wasn't what you would call a home with curb appeal, but the memories I hold from growing up here are quite wonderful. I skated on ice of the pig pond, chased cows, swung on the entrance gates and went on a delivery route through the small towns of Idaho with my father. We called the delivery route, "The Loop." I didn't know any other life and I loved the one that I had.

My brother and I were raised primarily by my dad because my mother passed away when I was six. It would be more correct to say that we raised ourselves except for a few exceptional people whom you will meet later in this story.

Right after my mom died, my father sent a telegram to my grandmother who left her very comfortable life in Florida to come to be with us immediately. Two years after she arrived, she suffered a stroke and we no longer had a "mother figure" in our lives. Dad did all he could to keep us together as a family. He managed to find one housekeeper after another who was charged with watching us.

We mostly did what we wanted and they kept the house, sort of. Even to this day, I remember many of their names and what they were like. There was Kelly Orr, Mrs. Barnhart, Edith Gilbertson, Dusty, Lucille, Mrs Cornell and then there was Ellen. It was Ellen Guiswite and her presence that was largely responsible for shaping my life.

Ellen was wonderful. She was like an angel that showed up in my life, and she came to our home from what seems now as an extraordinary circumstance. The prison warden had called my father and said that he had a homeless woman whose husband had been put in prison. Would he take her in to watch his children? My dad said, "Yes" and that is how Ellen became "ours" for two incredible years.

Ellen loved to laugh and taught me to play new and different games, and she was a wonderful cook. She walked with us on the riverbank of the Boise River. We rode the bus into Boise to watch movies. I often pass the spot near Borah Station Post Office in Boise and remember what it was like to stand on the corner with Ellen and wait for the bus.

At night, I would lay down beside her and it felt like a warm bean bag cushion. She would listen to me and tell me stories of high school and her family back in North Dakota. She made me feel safe and like a wonderfully secure child. Ellen gave me a great sense of security. As a child with very little that was secure, Ellen's presence and the love she offered me was life shaping.

When her husband Ray was released they moved away and that was the last that I saw of her. As I moved through life, grew up, married and raised children I often thought of Ellen. I told my husband and my children about the impact Ellen had on me and of her kindness.

More than fifty years passed. One day when my husband was sitting at his computer, he asked about Ellen and mentioned that it might be possible to find her, and so he did. I was shocked that she was still alive. I made a call to locate her and now we keep in touch and have occasional conversations. I got the opportunity to thank her for her kindness. I learned that she been very successful in her life. She had moved back to North Dakota and raised three children of her own after Ray left for good. She still loved to laugh and tell stories.

You just never know what kind of impact you might have on a child or someone else, when your lives intersect…even if it is for a very short time.

These memories of Ellen remind me that you just never know what kind of impact you might have on a child or someone else, when your lives intersect…even if it is for a very short time. I am so thankful that Ellen, a woman who was homeless at the time, was the catalyst for giving me tremendous childhood memories.

Who would have known that this whimsical childhood would be the background for my life as a successful parent and professional artist? I now liken my daily attitude and life perspective to what it is like to paint a great picture. Painting is a process of problem solving that doesn't always turn out perfectly the first time. Sometimes the artwork doesn't even get finished and you go on to the next one. Life is the same way. You can't get stopped on those things that seem unresolved or negative. Keep your focus on the masterpiece.

Julie Day
Professional Artist
Boise, Idaho
208-343-4243

Boredom is a Choice

LIBERTY BARRETT, 16

BORING...I think that this word is way over used. In fact I am convinced that it is many people's...or at least most kids'...favorite word. Everything is always boring. They never want to do anything in life because they are sure it's going to be boring. It is just going to put them out of their sanity. But the real truth is that boredom is a choice, one that can only be made by you. No one can make you bored or un-bored...it is all up to you.

If you look up the definition of boring, you will see that the dictionary says something along the lines of "stimulating no interest or enthusiasm." From this definition you can understand what most people mean when they call something boring. It is just a short way to say, "this is something I don't want to do. I would rather do something else more interesting."

Well...you say...do you mean there has never been times when you wished you were doing something else? Haven't you ever been "bored to tears"? Of course there have been times when I would rather have done something else. But this fact did not let what I was doing become boring. The reason it did not become boring is because I had an intentional purpose for doing what I was doing...even if I did not think it was totally exciting. Believe me...I have a disease called "Basketball Fever." I'd always rather be on the court shooting some hoops. But reality is, if everything you are doing has a purpose you will not get bored doing it...even if it is not "totally cool" or your favorite activity.

Now you may wonder...how can it be my fault if I watched the sports game and it turned out pathetically, so I got bored? Or, I went somewhere with my parents, but there was no one my age to hang out with. And there was NOTHING to do. How can I help being bored...the circumstances make it boring. And the truth is that you can still not become bored if you make that time useful and have a purpose. But most people...especially young people like me, won't try to make their time meaningful. In fact, they usually go into the situation with the presumption that it is going to be horrible. There have been many situations when I have been places where it was not the most enjoyable time. Again it was not horrible because there was a reason and purpose for my being there and doing what I was doing. If you try hard enough (which I have found does not have to be very hard at all) you will find something profitable to do with your time, even if the situation screams at you otherwise.

I think a good example for kids is school. We always hear how horrible and boring school is...or assume it will be. If you then asked the same person if they think there is a reason why they are in school, they would most likely tell you they didn't know. Now if that person knew the goal and purpose of school was to inform and educate them, as well as to help them gain knowledge for all of life, then they may look at school quite a bit differently. This concept is not just true about school. It can be applied to every area of life. Understanding the significance of a certain activity can make it far more enjoyable in the moment.

Another really good example is our culture's obsession with video games....especially among young people. By constantly playing these games, young people create an unrealistic world for themselves they

Start making every moment count by making every moment have a purpose

think is "exciting". Then, they explain how everything else in life is "boring" when compared to the video game excitement. *How can they even know that it is not as exciting as real life?* Most of them have never taken the opportunity to live life. It would be easy for me to say that everything but basketball in my life is "boring". Basketball definitely has its place, but other things have important purposes as well. Remember, if it has a purpose, it is not "boring". It may be tedious, trying, or time-consuming, yet by identifying a purpose you will be empowered to not only endure, but rather enjoy an otherwise monotonous event.

Even adults use the excuse that they are "bored", maybe while they are at church, or on a long commute to work. I know myself that long commutes (like my ride to basketball practice…nearly an hour each way) can be made boring-free as you realize its purpose. Sometimes you'll even have to find or create a purpose. Boredom is a choice whether a person makes it consciously or not. Adults should set the example for younger people and children by choosing not to be bored. Use your creativity…get a life!

Start making every moment count by making every moment have a purpose. Go shoot some hoops. Begin by making an impact on other people's lives by showing them with your example that life does not have to be boring…it can be exceptional. Get out there and have an exceptional, boring free life!!

Liberty Barrett
Boise, Idaho
liberty@biblicalview.com

Big Ripples from Small Stones

TIMOTHY BURNS

RON AND I lingered in the ballroom, reminiscing about Pastor Dan's skillful leadership. The banquet room spilled over with people honoring Dan and rubbing shoulders with old friends. Years prior, Ron and I had settled into Dan's church. Ron's interest in missions had taken him to Guatemala. My love for my family kept me home involved in urban street ministry. Like a pond's surface stirred by a small stone, Pastor Dan's work changed our lives, and we passed on the ripples of God's grace to those within our own reach.

That morning, I listened to hundreds recount the same story. Our lives were changed by God's hands through Pastor Dan. We were not pressed into a predefined mold. Instead, Dan led us into a relationship with Christ, and then insisted that God held an individual calling for each. There were no cookie cutters in Dan's ministry tool basket; yet his heart-seeking questions couldn't be evaded. "What do you think God wants you to do? God wants you to pass along his life, and love. How do you want to pursue his call on your life?" (See 2 Corinthians 5.17-18)

As I prepared to leave, the people speaking from the platform caught my attention. This couple had met in Dan's church, married and continued into seminary. They recently accepted the pastorate of a small congregation and their testimony concluded with this fact. Their story was repeated 33 times during Dan's 15 year ministry. Thirty three men and women, after finding a relationship with Christ, continued on into full time ministry. Ron and I looked at each other and nodded. We were among that company. I worked in the urban neighborhoods and streets a few blocks from the church doors while Ron caravanned shoes, food and building materials to orphanages in Central America.

While I marveled at the numbers, Ron's next few words arrested my perspective, and changed my heart. "You know, Dan's a good pastor . . . but not a great one. He doesn't preach all that well. You don't want to ask him to lead the singing. He is an average teacher who has trouble with large words." Having listened to Dan for over 10 years, I chuckled quietly as Ron continued. "No, Dan isn't great at anything. He's simply faithful. He loves God, trusts the Bible as God's true Word, and lives his faith. The people here are a testimony to what God will do through a faithful man."

Ron's intuitive words have rattled around in my mind and heart ever since. As someone who came to Christ in a time when Christian concerts and stadium-filling events are normative, I think I unconsciously looked for the 'big event.' Until that day, I had fallen into a trap . . . letting myself off the hook of living influentially for God today while I stood on the sidelines looking for something 'big' to do for Him, (or maybe to do for me).

As a result of that night, I made a new decision. I would focus my efforts on improving the spiritual life of one other person. I prayed and asked God to bring into my life one man whom I could bring into a relationship with Christ, help that person grow up in their faith, and then release into ministry. Like sowing seeds in a garden, and then nourishing those seeds until fruit was produced, I would cast my time, one at a time, into the life of one other person. At the end of the year, there would be two of us, and we would repeat the process. I couldn't speak to thousands, but within my grasp was winning one man, and then the two of us winning two more . . . and so on. In time, a faithful discipler can bring hundreds into the kingdom. In time, God can change the world through me, one person at a time, like Jesus did.

Like a pond's surface stirred by a small stone, Pastor Dan's work changed our lives, and we passed on the ripples of God's grace to those within our own reach.

Within a few months, I met Jon and through Jon, four more. We spent every Thursday night together for over two years. We dealt with divorce, temptation, forgiveness, personal holiness, and financial responsibility. We held each other accountable to ask tough questions and confront real life issues. "What does God want in my life? How can I be more a personal reflection of His love to the world that is at my front door? What is standing in the way of a deeper and more intimate, unconditional relationship with Christ?"

Today, I am humbled by how God moved in our small band of brothers. Three of the group have completed seminary. One oversees a ministry to divorcing couples. Another has accepted leadership over a small church. I published my first book on discipleship, character building and personal integrity. Another is taking the final classes to complete his ministerial accreditations. God worked through my faithfulness into these four men, who are now influencing hundreds of people I could never touch on my own . . . just like Dan's ripples in my pond.

This verse from the Bible reminds each of us how we can create a ripple effect. "Jesus gave (gifts to) some to be apostles; and some, prophets; and some, evangelists; and some, pastors and teachers. He gave these gifts for the perfecting (maturing) of the saints, that they do the work of ministering, so that the body of Christ is built up till we all attain . . . unto the measure of the stature of the fullness of Christ." (Eph 4.11-14)

Timothy Burns
Founder and Editor, Inkwell Communications
Author, *Forged in the Fire* (Hensley Publishing)
www.timothyburns.com
tim.burns@inkwellcommunication.com
Ph: 517-507-7030

Just Over the Edge

WINDI STEVENSON-GHRIST

We've been to the edge of grief and fear.
Completely helpless we've even gone over the edge,
headfirst into darkness … But we've never hit bottom …
Over the edge we've discovered a path – transparent
but solid, unseen but real … very, very real.
Like you, we too have often cried out, "Where's God?"
His answer is clear … "I'm here," he says. "Just over the edge."

~ Excerpt by Sheila Walsh from *Living Fearlessly*

MANY PEOPLE choose to live on the edge … pushing the limits of life in an attempt to avoid the mundane. Looking back, I realize that was my approach to life as I longed for my son, Hunter, to 'inherit' my love of the ocean. For me, growing up in southern California, there was nothing better than a day at the beach.

So with my two year old in tow, we headed off to the beach for his first encounter with the ocean. My intentions were good … to safely toss him around in the waves, expose him to the fun, and watch him fall in love with the Pacific. There was only one problem. Hunter did not fall in love. Instead, he developed a deep fear of water, horrified of the very thing that I loved most. I hated the thought of all that he would miss because of his fear. That is what fear does. It robs us of the best of life!

Sometimes we choose the edge and sometimes the edge chooses us. While I had chosen my love of the ocean, there have been a few fears in my life that have chosen me. In fact, at times I have felt that those fears have stalked me relentlessly, threatening to steal my best life.

My fears began early in life. I was intensely afraid of death and being alone as a child. These fears were eased by my younger sister, Casey. We shared a bond so strong that every memory from my childhood includes Casey being right by my side.

Casey was the kind of person who made all of life better…the sweet, shy, considerate one who always put others before herself. I was the kid on the edge, always pushing the limits. But she humored my overbearing personality and loved me just as I was. Life was good just because she was there!

Casey could say more with her smile than most could say with several sentences. I will never forget the last time she flashed me that smile. On July 26th, 1987, in a brief moment a speeding car came over the hill and swiftly swept my sister and her bike away during a triathlon that we were participating in together. I can still hear the crashing sound as she slammed into the windshield of the speeding car and the unmistakable thud of her body hitting the hot pavement beneath her. The smile that had always said so much just said "goodbye."

I knew that my entire life had completely changed. My greatest fear had just taken place before my eyes. Life had tossed me into the crashing waves of grief as I faced 'life after death' at 17. Casey was only 15.

The waves of uncertainty, fear and anger grew stronger and more out of control. Once again, I was drawn to the edge…the edge of reason. My thoughts spun out of control. If I had seen the car sooner, if I had refused to participate in that stupid race, if I had been a better sister while she was alive…endless 'what ifs' assaulted my heart and drove me to years of self destructive behavior.

Those years led me to the edge of strained family relationships, giving in to abuse, drugs and a defeated attitude. The best of life was passing me by. I knew Casey would have wanted me to live well for both of us…but I was too lost to find my way.

In more recent years, I managed to find joy in being a mom while married to a man I adored. Life was good, at least on the surface, and I was expecting my third child. But the memories of Casey lingered on, always reminding me of all I had lost rather than all I had to be grateful for. Underneath the surface, I was in bondage to the fear and disappointment of the past. I lived as if I was waiting to die rather than dying to really live.

On July 26th, 2003, the 16th anniversary of Casey's death (and in many ways, my own), I was rushing around with my daughter MacKenzie in the back seat of the car, making arrangements for her first birthday party. This day always brought sadness and reflection. Where was my life headed?

Then my ultimate wakeup call came in the form of an enraged driver on a California freeway. Out of nowhere, a young man drove quickly by me, furious that I had gotten in his way. He passed me, pulled abruptly into my lane and slammed on his brakes, leaving me nowhere to go. I attempted to steer around him, but instead clipped his bumper…sending my car out of control while he continued toward his planned destination. He did not stop. He just went on with his day.

My day, my life, did not go on. My car flipped onto its top and slid to an abrupt stop. It was all I could do to fight to stay conscious and alive for MacKenzie, as well as to make sure the emergency personnel

I lived as if I was waiting to die rather than dying to really live.

knew I was pregnant. My mission kept me alive and alert.

While still in the emergency room, a woman came in with a basket of teddy bears, giving two of them to my husband and my mother, one for MacKenzie and one for my unborn daughter. They wore t-shirts that exclaimed, "My name is Casey. It means brave and strong."

Even though the doctors doubted that it would be possible to save us both, my family felt God speaking to us with the reassurance that my daughter would survive…and her name would be Casey. It was as if Casey was there with me, willing me to 'live well' for both of us.

Only four days into my hospital stay, I was faced with the news that I was paralyzed. My choice to live was no longer just about me. I had to choose life if my unborn daughter was going to have a chance at life. All these years, I thought I would rather die than live without Casey. But the desire to live welled up within me. My choice to live was rewarded when my healthy baby was born.

I have just spoken with my son, Hunter. He spent the day with a friend at the beach. Now nine, he decided to conquer his fear of the ocean. He did not get rid of his fear, but rather, he got into the water with his fear tagging along. He discovered that he loves the ocean and cannot wait to show me his new boogie boarding skills. You might say he has surfed over his fear.

Life since my injury has not been easy. But as I listened to my son's excitement over conquering his fear, I was inspired to a new life perspective. I have lived in bondage to fear too long, worried what the next day would bring.

Well, the next day has come, and it has brought with it great loss. But it has also brought three beautiful children, new friends who encourage me to embrace life fully, and a growing awareness that it is my legacy to live well for me...for Casey...and for my children.

The edge of grief may have chosen me. But now, I choose the edge of my exceptional life, diving in with all that is in me. Fear tags along, but will not hold me in bondage any longer. I have been to the edge, fallen over the edge...and survived! With God beside me, I have tapped into strength I never knew I had.

Trust your best and refuse to be paralyzed by fear. Tap into your strengths and be guided by your faith. Therein lies the great adventure of life. I live mine from this wheelchair as Hunter lives his from his boogie board. How will you live yours?

Windi Stevenson-Ghrist
Mom of Three
Granada Hills, California
summerbreezy1970@yahoo.com
310-628-3815

Fearless

DOROTHY HOBERT

AS I gazed at the deep blue water, sunlit diamonds danced over the surface. Boats were all over the lake, and I saw families enjoying the holiday. My thoughts turned to my dreams – some yet to be fulfilled and many already accomplished. Great experiences await in life for those who choose to conquer their fears and follow their dreams. Experience has taught me that fear is but a stepping stone. Following are three personal stories of fears, dreams and exceptional times in my life.

I now live in my father's family's home, built by my great grandparents a century ago…a most unique experience! While living here I have had to face many fears, such as the fear of how I will pay for, care for, and preserve this aging home. As I was growing up, my family lived just down the street from this house. At five, I used to pick my grandmother's flowers and walk a block to trade them to the lady at the corner store for candy until my mother got wise to my being an entrepreneur. Growing up and being named after both of my grandmothers, I knew I was special. As I grew older, I realized that I had been chosen to carry on those family names.

My dreams have become warm reality as each year the trees bud out in new leaves and the flowers open in color. I know caring for this home is now my responsibility. As I awaken each morning, I know it is a new day to shine, to do my best and live my dreams. When the burdens get too heavy, I have my glorious Heavenly Father who tells me to give it all to him. Ahhhhhhhhh - one less fear!

As we drove to the cemetery, my head felt overwhelmed with fears. Now as I think back, those fears were so silly, but that day they seemed so big and so real. What would I discover as we went in search of my dream to find my grandmother's grave? I had only known her through a few pictures and the stories passed on to me by my mother and aunts. You see, my mother's mother was very ill with tuberculosis as a young woman. Dying at thirty-four, she was robbed of watching her children grow up. None of them knew exactly where she was buried.

If you will allow yourself to be open to new, sometimes surprising offers, you can live your dreams and gather joy as you discover a no-fear, dream-fulfilling journey.

Dear friends in Arizona invited me to come stay with them for a few days, making the trip to find my grandmother's grave possible. I had shared with them my dream of finding where my grandmother was buried. We went searching and it didn't take long to have a phone call returned with a response of "I think I found your grandmother's grave." All those irrational fears loomed in my head as we drove to the cemetery. I wanted my grandmother to be in a most beautiful place. The white block walls gave way to the green, well cared for beauty. Palm trees lined the roads. I was overwhelmed and teary eyed with joy and relief. As I left with copies of all the information and lots of pictures of grandma's gravesite, I knew I had to share this new knowledge with my mother and her siblings.

As Christmas approached, I decided to make all five of them a special present, an envelope of precious details about their mother. As they opened my gift to them, the grateful and tender responses touched my heart deeply. What if my fears had been so great that I had never given myself permission to live that dream? My joy and blessings would have gone unknown.

Special joy abounds for my aunt who was only one and a half-years old when her mother passed away. For my aunt's sixty-fifth birthday, her husband honored her with a headstone for her mother's gravesite. Our whole family treasures this gift. Never really having had a chance to know her mother, I am sure she can hardly wait until she is able to give her a big hug in heaven.

My quest paved the way for my Auntie Joyce, next to the oldest, to be the first sibling to visit her mother's gravesite in Arizona. As she returned home she bubbled over with feelings. I received a phone call from her. As we laughed and cried, we reminisced about stories and events she remembered about her mother. She told me, "Because of you, we know where our mother is now. Thank you, my darling niece." Fear is so small compared to the joys we have as we share our dreams. It has been amazing to watch several generations of this family be blessed by one simple act.

Stepping into a small airport waiting area last year, I had no idea of fears that would soon crowd my mind because I was in the right place at the right time. About four or five people were seated waiting for their planes. I sat down across from a young woman. We struck up a conversation. I don't remember what we talked about, just everyday ordinary things. Before we left on our planes we exchanged business cards. Much to my surprise about ten days later, I received an envelope with an invitation to be a co-author in a book project she was directing. I was honored but did not think it was something I would ever do.

Inside my head a little voice kept saying, " You have so many stories in here, pick one and write."

When I began writing my story, I felt like I had just started pre-school and she wanted me to do college. It made my knees shake and my stomach roll in complete chaos. After many hours of my brain doing battle over what I might have to offer in a story, the decision was made to begin. Fear was in full force now. What was I doing? I can tell stories all day long, as can most hairdressers, but write it down? That was scary. I am sure my fingers were cramped from rewriting that first story so many times. Oh, and this new language of writing and publishing, it is all Greek to me. Following my dream, walking through that huge fear and one book to my credit later, I am here again doing a second, and who knows how many more. All I can tell you is total joy, fulfillment and a whole wonderful new world of friends, excitement, and opportunities have opened up to me.

If you will allow yourself to be open to new, sometimes surprising offers, you can live your dreams and gather joy as you discover a no-fear, dream-fulfilling journey. This big, beautiful world is just waiting for you to embark and experience your exceptional life. Conquer your fears and give yourself permission to expand your world. Make the necessary changes to watch your dreams come true.

Dorothy Hobert
Greenacres, WA
509-926-6343
katie_hobbit@hotmail.com
www.dreamwithpassion.info

Die with your boots ON!

ANSON R THOMPSON

JOHN SUMMERS is a "good ol' boy." He was born in Tennessee, raised on hard work, meat and potatoes. When John started a concrete business in Muncie, Indiana, it came as no surprise to anyone that it would become extremely successful. Every day John labored alongside his employees - setting forms, working the concrete, and managing his business. Then one evening, just two months after John's 62nd birthday, he began having chest pains.

Somehow, he drove himself to the hospital, and after many tests the prognosis was grim. The doctors didn't think he would make it through the night. He did make it through that night and recovered well enough to go home, but his heart was in very bad shape. The doctors estimated he had lost 80% usage of his heart. At the time of his release, John could barely walk. After 62 years as the picture of health, this robust "superman" was primarily confined to his bed. But slowly his body began to recover, his spirit ever determined to thrive, and he returned to a somewhat normal life helping his wife Betty around the house, visiting his office, and managing his employees. Still, the fact that he could no longer "work" was driving him crazy. After much thought, he made up his mind. After forty-three years in the concrete businesses, John decided to sell his company to some of his employees and retire.

Not long after his retirement John became aware of an increasingly persistent pain in his back. Once again he was back in the hospital, this time for major back surgery. The surgery was a success and he soon found himself at home recuperating again, walking with the help of a cane and getting around fairly well, or so he thought. During his next trip to the doctor, he was told that he had developed a hernia, and it would require surgery. Over the next six months, John found himself back in the hospital two more times, once for the hernia operation and then knee surgery. It seemed as if his knees had held a meeting and agreed one of them would "go out" so they wouldn't be left out of all the extra fun and attention!

Two years later, John was sixty-four years old, fully recovered from all his surgeries, and he felt great. His exercise program included light weight training and a walk every other day. He began working on his rental properties, mowing the yard, and helping his wife with the groceries. At a routine follow-up appointment with his doctor, he was feeling stronger than he had for months.

As the doctor began his examination, John asked, "Doc, can I mow the yard?" "No, John." "Ok," said John, "but can I work on my rental properties?" "No, John," was again the response. "Well then, Doc, can I help Betty with the groceries, you know carry them in once she gets home?" The doctor, looked John straight in the eye said, "John, you have the same heart today that you had when you walked out of the hospital two years ago. If you insist on doing these things you will die of a heart attack. Now, I know you have many grandchildren. Why don't you go home, take off your shoes and relax. Watch TV, take it easy, hire someone to do those jobs and enjoy the next 20 years of life?"

John smiled and left for home thanking the doctor for his advice. When he got home his wife asked him, "Honey, what did the doctor

John might live 20 days or 20 years, but when it's John's time, he's determined he'll leave with his boots ON!

say?" With a somewhat devilish smile and renewed determination, John answered her, "The doctor said it was time for me to decide if I wanted to die with my boots on…or my boots off. Well, I've been thinking about that, and I've decided I'm going to get busy living and make sure I die with my boots on!"

And that's exactly what he does to this day. Every day he takes a two mile walk before leaving for work at his rentals, mow a yard, or help his wife with the groceries. John might live 20 days or 20 years, but when it's John's time, he's determined he'll leave with his boots ON!

Anson R Thompson
CEO, The Thompson Group
www.thethompsongroup.net
1-800-886-6655

Better Than Your Dreams

ELYSSE BARRETT

I'M A dreamer. I dream during the day and at night. Yet, while most people would call me a visionary, I also try to be as practical as possible. Sometimes in all this practicality, I forget about my dreams. In junior high and high school, I pictured my life as I thought it would be…the way that I wanted it to be. My life script would have been fairly typical if I had written it…graduate from high school, continue pursuing my passion of speaking, writing, and making a difference for Christ, and hopefully sooner rather than later, get married and raise a family. Since the age of eight, my deepest desire has been to become a stay-at-home wife and mother. Even though I do enjoy persuing the passions that God has placed on my heart, I have never aspired to be a woman with a professional career.

So, here I am dreaming about the exceptional life I WILL have. I continually thought of how happy I would be when I realized those dreams. But then I graduated and six months passed, then twelve, then eighteen, and I started to wake up!

It's been a long day. The phone was constantly ringing. On the way home, I figured that if I only return half of the e-mails I typically receive in one day, then I will be very behind before I know it. All is forgotten as I put the car into park and turn to see two of my little brothers running out of the house at full speed, arms wide open to give me big bear hugs.

As I am having all my breath squeezed out of me at the mercy of two sets of little arms, it suddenly dawns on me, this is an exceptional moment!

As much as I love my dreams, I have resolved to hold them loosely. I can't see the future, only God can. He is a loving, gracious God who has promised to do only that which is best for us. Sometimes all we see are the clouds, but He is above them.

My arms are around her, as she sobs and clings to me. She has been abused, rejected, and forgotten more times than she can remember. Even though she has now found a loving home, it still hurts. When it is all over, she gives me a tight squeeze. I will never forget the smile on her face and sparkle in her eyes as she walked out of the room.

Sometimes our exceptional moments come in ways we would never dream of.

Oh no, I have missed a phone call! The voice mail turns out to be a dear friend leaving a few encouraging words. My computer gives me the familiar "you've got mail" beep, and it turns out to be an e-mail from a friend I haven't heard from in a long time.

I discover that technology is a wonderful blessing to create and remember exceptional moments.

I look down the aisle as the scent of the fresh roses in my bouquet tickles my senses with the inevitable smell which emanates through weddings. My tears are tears of joy as I catch a glimpse of the beautiful bride on her father's arm.

Sometimes exceptional moments are once-in-a-lifetime…

They know that I'm not their mama. She's away on a trip and won't be back for a few more days. I'm trying to be a good substitute, but try as I might, mama still does it better!! Despite my efforts, they still give me good morning hugs and their eyes sparkle as we walk hand in hand.

...and sometimes exceptional moments may seem very ordinary.

As I share the story of my life and challenge the young people in the audience to decide that each of their lives has a purpose, that each of them can choose to live an exceptional life, sometimes all I get are blank stares...and looks that tell me I am droning on too long. As I try to make my words a little more exciting, I offer up a quick prayer that each person

As much as I love my dreams, I have resolved to hold them loosely. I can't see the future, only God can.

in the audience will be able to hear my passion and capture just a little bit for themselves. However, it seems hopeless. I continue to tell stories, weave in life principles, and silently pray. Just as I'm closing I scan my familiar audience, and see just a glimmer of passion lighting up in a few eyes. Over the next few days, they see that I am committed to "walk the walk," not just "talk the talk." Before they leave the event, a passionate fire to make a difference in the world can be seen in their eyes.

Sometimes exceptional moments are hard work...

It was the first leg of a long flight home and despite my usual exuberance to travel, I was already looking forward to my own shower, bed and pillow. I slowly wove my way to my assigned seat and sat down. I quickly made sure my stash of gum was within easy reach for the take off. Soon a voice broke through my fog, as I heard, "Ma'am, I think my seat is next to yours." He was certainly not the profile of someone I would have picked to share my leg room with, but the ticket stub was unquestionable. It WAS his seat. Deciding to be pleasant, we chatted. He was traveling, strictly on business; I was for business and pleasure. He wished that his job allowed him to enjoy creation. He was looking forward to getting home, as was I. He missed his family and so did I. Then, we started our descent, and I grabbed my package of gum. Out of the corner of my eye, I saw him glance at the package and noticed that he was in some discomfort. So, I said, "Would you like a piece or two?" As I glanced up, I saw that his eyes were pooled with tears as he said, "Yes, thank you." After a few moments of silence, he continued, "Do you know that no one has ever been as nice to me as you have in the last few minutes? What made you be so kind to me? You are not like anyone I have ever met before." Just before the plane touched down, I told him of the hope that was within me because of my savior, Jesus. He saw Jesus, not me. I hope and pray that he carries those words with him wherever his travels take him. I certainly continue to carry gum everywhere I travel.

…and sometimes they sit down in the seat next to you.

Reflecting on the past few years strengthens me as I refuse to live an ordinary life. In fact, I don't even allow that word in my vocabulary. Every moment I try to hold my dreams loosely, hold tightly to God's best life, and live a life of exceptional moments. Every exceptional moment is an important part of my exceptional life. While my dreams are still important, choosing to live an exceptional life now does not take anything away from them.

Take the time to live exceptional moments. Before you realize it, your life will be filled with exceptional moments…your life will be exceptional.

Sometimes your life can be better than your dreams. Mine is every day…every moment!

Elysse Barrett
President, America's Renewal
Author, Speaker, Event Facilitator
208-377-2364
ebarrett@americasrenewal.com
www.americasrenewal.com

A Standing Ovation

JENNIFER OPPEL

"All the world is but a stage…"
~ William Shakespeare

I THINK most of us, at least once in our childhood, found ourselves dressed in a hand-made, silly costume, performing before an audience of proud parents and grandparents, reciting a memorized line or singing with the choir. My earliest memory of this was as a lamb in a church musical. I can vaguely recall the costume consisting of a paper bag with a face-sized hole cut out and covered in cotton balls. For many, this is where our off-off-off-Broadway career begins and ends. Except for a few subsequent (and equally memorable) times, I know mine almost did. But then the most wonderful thing happened. I ended up in a class I could not stand my very first year in high school.

After two short weeks I ran to my guidance counselor frantic and was offered a transfer to one of the few classes not already full…stage-craft. I didn't really know what it was at the time but with a grateful heart and without hesitation I declared, "I'll take it!" And just like that, a whole new world opened up to me; props, set design and construction, lighting and later acting. The friendships made those four years endure still today. It promoted creativity, confidence and a sense of responsibility and teamwork. Only with everyone working together with a clear goal in mind did we then all share in the success.

Since then my "staring role" has been to leave the footlights to start my own company as a Business Consultant and Virtual Assistant, capitalizing on my fourteen years of experience as an Executive Administrator. I now help "set the stage" for other professionals, putting all the necessary "props" at their disposal, editing "scripts" and putting them in the best possible "light" to ensure a successful "production" from "opening night through the run of the play." "Setting the stage" with props and sets lead to the same attention to detail when designing systems or working with a business to implement a vision, project or completely new business opportunity.

High school theater was an unexpected answer to prayer and prepared me for my eventual career:

THEATER:	TODAY:
Prop Chief – Finding the perfect item and organizing props necessary to support the actor's performance. Standing behind the scenes, ready to provide them on cue.	Cyber-Secretary/Research Assistant – Collecting and organizing data and spearheading special projects with an attention to detail.

> **It promoted creativity, confidence and a sense of responsibility and teamwork. Only with everyone working together with a clear goal in mind did we then all share in the success.**

THEATER:	TODAY:
Costuming/Makeup – Research to determine the most appropriate "look" and tailoring it to be the most flattering to the individual actor.	Business Consulting – Working with corporate personnel on everything from marketing to management to promote a "winning image."
Lighting – Using colors, shadows and intensity to set the right mood and illuminate the actor in the best and most appropriate light possible.	Creative Consultant – Using tools like PowerPoint and the Web to illuminate otherwise flat facts in a way that they are both clear and memorable.
Set Design/Construction – Providing suitable background images. Surrounding the actors with images of locations that help transport the audience with the actor to the desired place and time.	Systems Analyst – Building systems that save time and money that provide a perfect backdrop to success including profit center self-insurance for builder/developers and self-perpetuating office systems.
Acting – Learning to perform a role in conjunction with others with believability and enthusiasm, improvising whenever necessary.	Virtual Assistant – Working in tandem with other professionals to produce a viable finished product; projecting the message as the client wants it heard.

And most importantly, while we each may play many "roles," I have found that for the highest level of performance, God is the ultimate Director. Through prayer he gently guides our preparation, teamwork and diligent efforts to carry out His will. Remind yourself that His plans are so much farther-reaching than our own. So next time you find yourself in a class (or situation) you can't stand or when you begin to doubt, seek out that elusive opportunity hidden within your challenge. With proper commitment, effort and perseverance your performance is sure to get a standing ovation.

Jennifer Oppel
CEO-Solutions Made Easy
Stagehands to Your Success
208-571-7511
On the web at: www.IdeasOnUs.com
Email: SolutionsMadeEasy@yahoo.com

The Sky is No Limit

MERCY HOPE

MY LIFE has NOT been a tale of someone who "pulled herself up by her own bootstraps." The life I'm living and the amazing opportunities I've been given are truly gifts from God. Because of the odds I faced growing up, including poverty, homelessness, and domestic violence, I was one of the "least likely to succeed." There were many nights when I thought I wouldn't live to see another sunrise.

Traveling the country, working for a national ministry, and interviewing influential personalities was certainly never something that I would have dreamed of doing. But today, my perspective is: the sky is no limit!

It has now been five years since I conducted my first interview. My initial experience was backstage with a beloved veteran gospel recording artist. My next opportunity came the very next day, sitting on a couch in a posh hotel lobby with a young pop singer who quickly became a household name in Contemporary Christian music. Both interviews were a great success and I was stoked! They were first published in *An Encouraging Word* magazine, for which I am a regular columnist.

The Lord continued to open doors for my interviews. One key experience was connecting with a woman who works for a major record label. She put a good word in for me with the staff at the record company. They in turn connected me with key people in the industry. They went so far as to work alongside me at events and conventions. Not only did they provide invaluable practical help, but their actions bolstered my morale and showed they believed in what I was trying to do. I was blown away by the support shown to me.

In 2003 www.FaithTalks.com was launched. Today the media resource, FaithTalks.com has become a well-respected source of inspiration for women around the world! My first exclusive FaithTalks.com interview was in September of that year. As I sat talking with the President of the largest public policy women's organization in the United States, I had to literally pinch myself to make sure I wasn't dreaming! How could someone with my background be discussing the key challenges facing our country today with this national leader, someone who I perceived to be out of my league. I certainly didn't have the long list of credentials or professional achievements that many who she could have met with that night had. But when God is setting up the itinerary, the sky is no limit. I've laughed, cried and prayed with people who I never would have imagined even meeting. Some of them I now have the privilege of calling my friends.

So, how is it that I find myself in such a privileged position? What took me from being a victim to a victor? Is it self-confidence and mere positive thinking? No. In fact, all my life I've battled insecurity. In a culture where "Image is everything," I would be an image consultant's nightmare. The only viable answer is: the favor of God. Every good thing in my life is because of Jesus Christ.

I met Jesus when I was nine years old. He looked past my confident façade and saw a broken little girl who desperately wanted to be loved and accepted. He empowered me with His Holy Spirit and set me on a course that has led me to where I am today. So is my life a bed of roses? I would say that pretty well describes it: incomparable beauty in the midst of numerous painful thorns. I've had my share of disappointments. We all face obstacles. There are no exemptions - life is hard. In Michigan, where I currently reside, they would say, "It takes grit." In the great state of Texas they call it, "havin' guts." I'm not one of those people who just want to "make it through" life. I want to give it all I've got! I'm committed to following Jesus no matter what!

I'm not one of those people who just want to "make it through" life. I want to give it all I've got!

Often, I've had to let go of my dreams to embrace my true purpose. Sometimes God says "No" to what I think would be a good thing. Just like a wise and loving father, He knows what is BEST. But my life, and work, would mean nothing if I am not fulfilling the mission for which I was created. Each of us were uniquely formed in our mother's womb by the Hand of God for a specific destiny, and we can choose to embrace it or throw away our most valuable resource – our life.

One of my mom's favorite verses in the Bible is Proverbs 3:5-6, which says, "Trust in the Lord with all your heart; don't trust in your own understanding. Seek His will in everything you do, and He will give you direction." Have you sought His direction for YOUR life? Have you allowed Him to empower you to fulfill your destiny? There is no such thing as an impossible mission when you are truly trusting Jesus.

I've had people approach me with questions like, "I saw you having lunch with that big name news anchor yesterday. How do you know him?!" or "How did you get an interview with so-and-so? I've been trying forever to meet that person!" At times, they're hoping that I can get them an "in." But the bottom line is, if you don't know me you haven't missed much. And if you never meet your heroes you'll survive, but if you don't know Jesus, you are really missing out on life itself. It's when you surrender your dreams, goals and plans to Jesus, and tell Him, "I'll do what You want me to do" (because faith walks) "I'll say what You want me to say" (because faith talks) "I'm Yours, so have Your way in my life," the sky is no limit!

Mercy Hope
Interviewer, FaithTalks
www.faithtalks.com

New Hope

KIM FLETCHER

"Steward the prayers that have already been answered."
~ Pastor Wayne Cordeiro
New Hope Christian Fellowship
Honolulu, HI

WHEN DOES the truly exceptional life begin? When we find true love, when we reach our business goals, when we make a few lasting friends, when we own our dream vacation home?

If this is the only principle by which we measure obtaining a truly exceptional life, then many of us would be left chasing a dream that may never be fully realized ... leaving us living a 'less than exceptional' life. In my search for an answer to the question as to when - or even if - my exceptional life would begin, I tripped upon an unexpected answer in an unexpected place.

A couple of years ago, I sat in a crowded school building on a Sunday morning in Honolulu, Hawaii, surrounded by the members of a church known as New Hope. The service was rich with Hawaiian tradition and a passionate message from a pastor named Wayne Cordeiro.

The essence of the message that sunny Hawaiian Sunday could be summed up in one statement made by Pastor Wayne. He exclaimed that we should "Steward the prayers that have already been answered." A steward is a manager by definition. So he was actually challenging us to make the most of the great blessings that have already come our way.

He went on to say that most of us go through life looking for, asking for, and wishing for the next thing with little attention to the vast riches that have already been given to us. In other words, people have a tendency to want what they do not have and to not want what they do have. We fail to be intentionally grateful for what is already present, often losing sight of the people and things of greatest importance.

In my search for an answer to the question as to when – or even if – my exceptional life began, I tripped upon an unexpected answer in an unexpected place.

That afternoon, surrounded by the surf and sun, I pondered that powerful thought. Do I personally manage well what has already been entrusted by God into my life? What am I doing with what I have?

My mind drifted back to the East Coast to the original home of my maternal grandparents … Ernest and Dorsie Hartley. While their physical lives have passed, their spiritual lives continue to impact my life daily.

You see, it would be impossible for me to think about my personal definition of the 'exceptional life' or all I have been given without thinking of them…two people whose lives were marked by kindness, gentleness, love and loyal devotion. Two people whose lives were marked by the power of prayer.

Ernest and Dorsie would have been called ordinary by many standards. Their home was simple, their bank account was only adequate, their clothes had no labels, and their lives were marked by simple hard work and devotion to only two objectives...faith and family.

They were stone deaf at rather early ages...you know, the kind of "hard of hearing" that allows the people in the nearby county to overhear your conversation. So, as a child, I made a game of sneaking into their home (their home was only one house away from my home) and seeing how long I could be inside before they detected the 'intruder'.

One particular night, I managed to sneak in undetected after dark. Under the radar of their poor hearing, I lingered in the kitchen...creeping ever closer to the living room. I drew close enough to hear their voices. I tuned my ears (glad I didn't inherit that bad hearing...yet!) to hear their conversation. But they did not sound as if they were talking to one another. Who were they talking to?

I peered into the living room. There they were...kneeling down side by side with their elbows propped close together on a favorite chair. They were praying. And as I listened, I realized that they were going name by name through the family names...over 50...praying for each with passion.

I left silently but differently...they never knew I overheard them. I did not understand fully but somehow I realized that those prayers day after day, side by side, of two hearts united in asking God to bring blessing, protection and His purpose to each life in their family would have a lasting impact.

They did not hear me but I was certain that God did hear them.

Years later, after my grandfather's death, I was spending the night in that same simple white cottage as my grandmother recovered from surgery. My bed was in the same room where those prayers had been echoed over the years. 'Granny' was just a short distance away in her own room...close enough to be heard if she needed me. She was weak and frail. Her voice had faded from strong to soft and wispy.

Almost asleep, I heard her call my name. I awakened quickly, thinking she needed me. I waited as I then heard other names. The once strong voice, now thin and wispy, was still praying that same prayer for each member of her family...without her husband of 64 years, without the ability to kneel, without the luxury of health or youth...but with the power of knowing she would always be heard by the One she had called upon for over 85 years.

I was silenced, stunned, and shaped...a weak frail woman, worthless to the world, was shaking Heaven on my behalf.

My exceptional life did not begin as a result of any of my human efforts, college degrees, great friends, passionate spirit or compassionate heart. My exceptional life began with those who chose to plead with God for His Best for me even before I had the good sense to know what was best for me.

So today, I 'steward' that exceptional life. It is not my job to create it but rather to manage it...to love those people God places in my life, to live in integrity, to develop my gifts and talents in an attempt to leave the world better than I found it. And to one day have someone (if not many people) say that they are now living their exceptional life because, before they could see God's greater vision for themselves, I was already pleading with God to bring His Best into their lives.

I have been given much as a result of the invisible impact of prayer. Perhaps your exceptional life has already begun. All you need to do now is to recognize it, embrace it, and ask yourself what you can do to impact others with what you have already been given. Stop searching and start living!

Kim Fletcher
Life Coach, Professional Speaker, People Development Innovator
CEI-Creative Life Navigation
International Director-Life Compass
Creating Personal Vision Clarity for clients and audiences worldwide
828 327 6702
kimfletchercoach@aol.com
www.creativelifenavigation.com

Your Exceptional Life Begins Now

~ Co-Author Biographies ~

TAMMY ADAMS

Tammy Adams would be described by her family and friends as loyal, humorous, light-hearted, and fun loving. It is no mistake that she has served the world of physical rehabilitation with excellence for nearly 20 years as a physical therapist assistant. Encouraging and assisting others comes naturally for this woman of faith. As an author and contemporary Christian vocalist, Tammy encourages her readers and her listeners to embrace the best of life NOW, rather than focusing on what has not yet come to be. She and her husband Dennis make their home in Hickory, North Carolina. They have one child in the Lord, Alex.

ELYSSE BARRETT

Elysse Barrett is the President of America's Renewal (www.americasrenewal.com), a service that provides speakers and organizations with resources to have a more effective impact. As a twenty year old young woman, she is an accomplished speaker and writer who is passionate about impacting her generation to make a difference for Christ! She is active in her family's ministry (www.biblicalview.com) as well as many other culturally relevant local and national organizations. Elysse's hobbies including making friends, traveling, collecting inspirational stories, writing, speaking, and encouraging others. As the oldest of seven, Elysse's greatest love is her family. She spends much time with them, and looks forward to getting married and having a family of her own. Her goal every day is to passionately pursue God's best life.

LIBERTY BARRETT

Liberty Barrett is sixteen years old and lives an exceptional, boring-free life with her awesome parents and six siblings. They currently reside in Boise, Idaho. She loves sports and is specifically passionate about basketball. Liberty makes it her lifetime goal to live as a hero (one who encourages, inspires, and challenges others in their walk with Christ) to many. Right now she is a full-time student who loves to spend her time being a friend. Liberty's biggest aspiration is to eventually establish a Children's Home where those in troubled situations will learn to overcome, live, laugh, love, and find hope in Christ. Liberty has already begun discovering how this is accomplished by involving herself in a Children's Home about an hour away from where she lives.

TINA SWANSON BROOKES

Tina Swanson Brookes lives to love others. Her favorites are her husband, Jim, and her three children: Joseph, Jon-Isaac and Jama. Tina also adopts many other children along the way. She works as a school counselor, volunteers as a church youth leader and has traveled extensively with students over the past five years. Her "family" has become quite large! Tina is a life long learner and has been blessed with the world's greatest friends! She is motivated and mentored by extraordinary people every day! The story that she has written for *Your Exceptional Life Begins Now* is the intro for her new book, *Ordinary People Living Extraordinary Lives* which will be released in 2007.

TIMOTHY BURNS

Timothy Burns writes for a diverse market of international clients. While personalities vary in size and shape, human nature does not. It's Timothy's ability to identify the human or cultural element that sets his work apart. His writing spans topics of Christian living, apologetics, and the hidden benefits arising out of personal difficulty. In the professional field, Timothy's insight into human dynamics is evident in many professional white papers. His first book, Forged in the Fire, follows numerous 'How To' articles for writers, contributions to MBA business projects, and consultation on IT soft systems transformation for a global manufacturing firm. Timothy can be reached via the web at www.timothyburns.com.

LINDA L BUTLER

Linda Butler lives in Greer, South Carolina. She has worked in manufacturing for over 18 years, beginning as production associate and is now a successful member of management. She obtained her education, earning a Master's degree in Human Resource Management from Clemson University, while working full-time. In her spare time she enjoys reading, writing poems, baking cakes and helping others. She uses her education and experience to coach those who are unemployed or underemployed. Her motto is "to whom much is given, much is required." Knowing that she has been blessed, she is passionate about being a blessing to others.

JULIE DAY

Julie Day was born and raised in Boise, Idaho. The place, the culture and the people are very close to her heart. Her career as a professional artist began when her husband, Jerry, brought home a set of paints after observing the sketches that she drew for their three children. Without formal training in art, she developed a style of her own and soon galleries began to call and request her work. The rest is history as she has sold over 3000 paintings all over the globe. Recently, she and Jerry purchased a home in the East End of Boise where she can walk to coffee shops and visit friends in a lifestyle that fits her perfectly.

SHARON DESJARLAIS

Sharon Desjarlais is a nationally certified Life Purpose and Career Coach who loves helping women in mid-career crisis discover and achieve their true calling. As an award-winning writer and editor for more than 20 years, she's experienced at marketing a wide range of businesses, from home-based to multinational. Now she's chosen to focus her career on her own life mission – to inspire, encourage and support creativity, empowerment and joy in women and children. She expresses that passion by offering workshops, one-on-one coaching and group coaching to women who want to work with joy. She also teaches literature and creative writing to junior- and senior high-school students in South Florida, where she lives with her husband Roy, daughters Devin and Nicole, and a dysfunctional boxer named Buster.

BOB EALING

Thirty five years (Ok . . . 7 states, 10 jobs, and 14 states later!) of business management and leadership have prepared Bob to lead others as they make exciting, life-changing decisions to "Move To The Edge!" His mission is to partner with businesses - and individuals - in developing skills to manage life and business more successfully. Bob brings exceptional leadership skills, engaging humor, and heartfelt compassion to all aspects of teaching, speaking, consulting, and life-coaching. Bob would like to work with you . . . even if you've lived and worked in the same place all your life! www.movetotheedge.com

BOB FLETCHER

Bob Fletcher spent most of his professional career serving as a highly respected insurance agent and dad who likes to fish and be with people. He transitioned into tile and marble design and installation in 1995. Major health issues related to his heart led to quadruple bypass surgery and a near death experience that heightened his desire to be intentional about health. Bob joined Ecoquest, International, a health-conscious company, as a distributor. Within the company, Bob provides leadership to an industry that is supplying healthy living technology, including state of the art air and water purification systems. Bob just celebrated his 43rd anniversary with his wife, Kay. Their daughter, Kim Fletcher, is the Co-Director of the *Don't Miss Your Boat* book series.

LORIE GARLAND

Lorie Garland is a native and resident of Hickory, NC. She received her BSBA with a concentration in Marketing and Economics from Appalachian State University located in the beautiful mountains of North Carolina. Employed by the Catawba County Chamber of Commerce, she is involved in many non profit organizations and serves on the boards of several associations through her motivational speaking and leadership, she strives to influence and empower women to step beyond their comfort zone both personally and professionally in order to live life to its fullest. She enjoys spending time with her husband, Bryant and her two children, Emma and Bryce. Top on her list of favorite things: her children's laughter.

JACKIE GEROSIN

Jackie Gerosin is a woman who lives with charisma and passion regardless of what life throws her way. She is a mom of two and senior loan officer in the mortgage industry. Her life revolves around her family, her friends and being active in the community. Doing a story in *Your Exceptional Life Begins Now* began as an "out of the comfort zone" experience for Jackie but one that she feels will be the catalyst for trying other challenging personal and professional experiences that lead to life filled with wonderful adventures.

WINDI STEVENSON-GHRIST

Windi Stevenson-Ghrist is a survivor. Windi has overcome many trials, but no matter what, she knows that she can survive. She holds tightly to the promise that God has a plan for her and her life - one that is full of many changes, many challenges, and many blessings. One of her greatest changes is learning to live life as a paraplegic, in a body that will not respond the way she would like. Windi's greatest blessing is being the proud mother of three beautiful children. Her greatest challenge is learning to accept that terrible events don't have to have terrible outcomes. Windi's goal in life is to trust God and remember there are no mistakes in God's world.

LISA HARPER

Lisa Harper is a 40 year-old pastor's wife and soccer mom who lives with her four children in the Detroit area. She has a Master's Degree in Reading from Eastern Michigan University and has been heavily involved in teaching, tutoring or homeschooling for nearly twenty years. Lisa's interests include piano, gymnastics, writing and public speaking. In 2003 Lisa founded Marathon Mission, a faith and community-based charity for walkers and runners that began at the Detroit Free Press/Flagstar Bank Marathon. To learn more about what makes Lisa tick, visit her at her website www.marathonmission.net.

DOROTHY HOBERT

Dorothy Hobert lives in Eastern Washington. A high spirit and passion for life surround her daily. Born the oldest of six children, she is a mother of three, and grandmother of four. Her treasures in life are family and friends. Dorothy's abundance of hobbies, including scrapbooking, sewing, quilting, gardening, entertaining, and traveling give delight in any spare time. A career of thirty-five years was spent in the beauty business, nine years in teaching photo journaling classes, and three years helping others find better health and financial freedom. Becoming an author, now of two books, has opened up a whole new avenue to travel. It has been a journey full of surprises, challenges and adventures for one country girl excited about life. www.dorothyh.familiesinfaith.com.

MERCY HOPE

Mercy Hope is a twenty four year old homeschool graduate who loves Jesus and the life He gives. She is an interviewer for www.faithtalks.com, as well as a regular columnist for *An Encouraging Word* magazine (www.anencouragingword.net). In addition to working in the Graphic Design Department for Wisdom's Gate (www.wisdomsgate.org), Mercy also serves as the Itinerary and Event coordinator for conference speakers, Skeet Savage and Israel Wayne. Mercy's passion is to share the hope she has found in Jesus Christ through writing, speaking, and one-on-one counseling. You can visit her official website at www.mercyhope.com

DIANNE HOUGH

Dianne Hough resides in Boise, Idaho where she is a top producing realtor for Group One. Having been born and raised in Idaho (as she puts it, "locally grown" like the potatoes) Dianne has a true appreciation for the quality of life found there. Her writing exemplifies her high energy approach to business, family and life! Dianne's positive outlook is infectious as she lives her slogan "I'm sold on Idaho!" Dianne and lifetime husband, Bob, have two grown daughters, Angie and Kristi. Together they enjoy hiking, biking, snow skiing and walks along the river with their big Alaskan Malamute, Kodiak.

STACY JAMES

Stacy James is a woman of passion and purpose... and interestingly, a woman whose 'life calling' was born out of her challenge of being faced with a disability following a diving accident. Stacy has gone on to develop a positive attitude, a deep reserve of faith, unthinkable courage, and perseverance. She shares these attributes with audiences worldwide as a speaker, author and accomplished wheelchair athlete. She is the Founder and Director of "Walking Victorious," a non-profit organization that equips people to rise above the challenges of life. Her website is www.walkingvictorious.com.

JANICE McMILLIAN

Janice McMillian is founder and president of J. Marie Concepts, which creates, manufactures and distributes handmade greeting cards and other written products. She is also founder of Zadok Publishing, a self-publishing enterprise which produces Christian, inspirational and motivational non-fiction books. Through a variety of literary formats, the message that Janice conveys in her books is that life is short and it is God's desire that you discover and walk in the divine purpose for your life. She is author and publisher of Let the Redeemed of the Lord, Say So and Bruised, Broken and Blessed, which is expected to be released by the fall of 2005. She knows her life mission is to "write books" that inspire, impact and transform the hearts of people to accomplish greater heights through their gifts, talents and abilities.

www.j-marieconcepts.com

JENNIFER OPPEL

Jennifer Oppel lived and worked in Southern California and Las Vegas before making the move to her current home in Idaho. She has over 15 years of experience in the corporate offices of various real estate industry leaders including Prudential, Americana Group, REALTORS®. She has held positions as an Executive Secretary, Administrative Assistant, Marketing Manager and Events Coordinator. In 2003, she started Solutions Made Easy, utilizing her experience to the benefits of others through creating turnkey systems, heading up special projects and improving overall office functionality. One of her current passions is assisting builder/developers and other companies set up profit center self insurance systems.

ANSON ROSS THOMPSON

Anson Ross Thompson is married to the most beautiful woman, Jodi, in Parker City, Indiana. Andy and Jodi have 2 children, son Tanner (10) and daughter Quincy Jo (8). Anson is also the CEO for The Thompson Group, an independent insurance agency, located in beautiful Parker City, Indiana. Anson entered the insurance business in 1992 after receiving his bachelor's degree in Insurance and his Masters degree in Information and Communication Sciences from Ball State University. The Thompson Group's mission statement is "Find the Pain, Heal the Pain, Show the Love."

CAROL WATSON, PhD

Dr. Carol J. Watson's greatest joys have been in challenging teens to dream BIG as they discover their potential and develop skills for living an exceptional life in a global community. She is a veteran high school teacher, speaker and author with a Ph.D. in Workforce Education and Development from Pennsylvania State University. In 2005 her speaking ministry expanded to include women's groups focusing on families, communication and leadership. Carol's speaking style is described as energetic, motivating and humorous. You can contact Carol at: cjw141@yahoo.com

JAMES A VOSSLER

Jim Vossler is the "Upward Mobility Specialist" for The Rainmaker Group, a group of gurus whose objective is maximizing possibility in organizations.

Jim's life experience has taken him from the classroom to the locker room to the boardroom.

Prior to joining The Rainmaker Group, Jim served as Director of the Harold Schafer Leadership Center at the University of Mary in Bismarck, ND, and as Education Director at a regional hospital.

Jim is an award winning Mathematics teacher and high school basketball coach and was singled out as one of "Five Outstanding Young North Dakotans." He has undergrad degrees in Physical Education and Mathematics, and Masters degrees in Mathematics and Management.

CHRISTOPHER YOUNG

Christopher Young is on a journey called life in Bismarck, North Dakota with his wife, Sandy, and his two children, Gracynn and Macauley, and a dog named Boo. Christopher is the Founder and Difference-Maker of The Rainmaker Group. Through The Rainmaker Group, Christopher helps people and organizations maximize their full potential at work and at home. Christopher's passions include his family, inspiring others to their fullest potential, and inspirational speaking across the United States. Christopher strongly believes everything happens on purpose and that we are all here to serve one another. Christopher graduated from North Dakota State University with an undergraduate and Master's degree in Economics.

Your Exceptional Life Begins Now

~ About the Directors ~

KIM FLETCHER

Kim Fletcher is passionate about life and it shows. Her enthusiasm and ability to connect with individuals from all walks of life are what set her apart as a Life & Business Coach, Speaker, and Author. Clients quickly refer to her as friend and organizations that hire her point to her as the one who reinforced enthusiasm while challenging them to work in integrity, gratitude, and personal accountability. She is a sought-after speaker who leaves audiences challenged and changed. Her coaching, speaking and writing bring lasting results to organizations, schools and companies of any size in the US and abroad.

Her ability to 'navigate the best course for all of life' began with herself, as she set out to take the best of her professional roles as physical therapist, college educator and disability advocate … blending them into a creative way to impact others. Kim brings first-hand experience to redesigning life around one's passions and strengths. Her unique coaching techniques and passionate speaking style allow clients and audience members to design strategies that bring life-changing breakthroughs.

Those breakthroughs include taking on new leadership roles, cultivating successful relationships, aligning your work with your strengths for greater peace and freedom, getting into advanced degree programs, moving beyond the limiting beliefs associated with disabilities and challenging people from all walks of life to embrace the value of each person, regardless of disability status.

As a People Development Innovator, she spends her days empowering others to live their best lives NOW! Her dedication to that empowerment was the basis for the concepts that became the foundation for this book. She is a creative genius behind the design and primary concepts for *Don't Miss Your Boat* and *Your Exceptional Life Begins Now.*

Kim shares these radical perspectives with her clients and audiences:

* Authenticity brings much greater freedom and impact
  than perfection
* The right perspective changes everything
* Personal vision is essential to life
* Authentic faith is the greatest 'Life Compass'
* It is never too late to create lasting change in your life and work.

Kim is CEI of Creative Life Navigation and the International Director of Life Compass, a non profit outreach that is dedicated to challenge and empower individuals affected by disability and others who long to catch the bigger vision for their lives.

Kim Fletcher
'Creating Personal Vision Clarity for clients and audiences worldwide'
Life Coach, Speaker, Author, Disability Expert
CEI – Creative Life Navigation
International Director- Life Compass
KimFletcherCoach@aol.com
www.creativelifenavigation.com
www.YourExceptionalLife BeginsNow.com

MARYANNA YOUNG

Maryanna Young has an excitement for life that is contagious. She believes that encouragement is key for others to live out their lives with excellence. Her background includes many years as an athlete, sports coach, personal fitness trainer, event director and business manager for professional athletes. She developed the concept for and co-founded the Idaho Women's Fitness Celebration, one of the largest sporting events for women in the US.

Her work has taken her around the world. She has worked with clients to build national media opportunities with organizations such as ESPN, NBC, CBS, ABC and companies such as Nike, Ocean Spray, United Airlines, Asics, General Motors, Key Corporation and Bank of America. She has experience managing and coaching small business owners, entrepreneurs, non profit organizations and executives, as well as professional and Olympic athletes.

She is President of Personal Value Coaching and CEO of the FMG Companies where she places a high value on assisting others in taking action on their life long vision. As a life and business coach, she enjoys implementing the simple strategies and action plans that move dreams into everyday reality. She is passionate about creating a coaching environment that allows individuals and companies to be wildly successfully.

Her clients are doing BIG things to merge their lives and their dreams such as opening new companies, launching non profit organizations, writing books, taking more vacations, supporting others in new ventures and spending valuable time with the significant people in their lives.

The *Don't Miss Your Boat* and *Your Exceptional Life Begins Now* Projects promote her enthusiasm to move individuals out of their comfort zone and into sharing significant messages with a broader audience. She believes that one critical area for motivational and inspiration is to highlight the stories of what she terms, everyday heroes. She loves the opportunity provided by these projects, to create a personal look into people's lives in addition to the stories that are widely broadcast via the TV, Radio and Internet media.

Recently she launched an educational resource called *Blank to Book: From Idea to Amazon in 150 Days*. Blank to Book shares invaluable secrets that allow anyone regardless of their writing ability to turn their ideas into books in a shorter time frame with less effort. She is passionate about educating and inspiring individuals to write the book that is inside of them.

Maryanna Young
"Helping ordinary people achieve extraordinary dreams"
Life and Business Coach, Speaker, Author and Friend
President – Personal Value Coaching
CEO – FMG Companies
personalvalue@aol.com
www.personalvaluecoaching.com
www.blanktobook.com
www.YourExcceptionalLifeBeginsNow.com

~ Acknowledgements ~

Many thanks to:

Our Co-Authors
who have opened their hearts, shared their stories
and strive everyday to live their lives in exceptional ways

Elysse Barrett
&
Michele Howe
for their wonderful editing assistance

Jennifer Oppel
for proofing page after page
as a service to your fellow Co-Authors

Nick Zelinger
at NZ Graphics for his creativity and patience
on the Interior Design and the Cover Design.
www.nzgraphics.com

David Hollander
the creative genius behind our website
and our book fulfillment
www.sparkweb.net

Many thanks to our collective families, friends, and co-workers
who stood by all of us in the writing and production process
of this project. We appreciate each one of you!

Begin living
your exceptional
life now...

Personal Coaching by phone for all budgets

Live Presentations to your audience

Kim Fletcher
Creative Life Navigation
Hickory, North Carolina
828-327-6702

Maryanna Young
Personal Value Coaching
Boise, Idaho
208-447-9036

Want to hear a Co-Author's story up close and personal?

Many of the Co-Authors have dynamic presentations to share with your company or organization.

Contact information is provided at the end of each chapter.

Need a speaker recommendation?
Contact Maryanna Young,
personalvalue@aol.com

Get the speaker that picks up where the book leaves off.

Yes! I would like Kim Fletcher to speak for my organization.

Name: _____

Organization: _____

Event Name: _____

Event Date: _____

Your Phone: _____

Your Email: _____

Contact Kim Fletcher
828-327-6702
KimFletcherCoach@aol.com

~

Fill out this form online at
www.CreativeLifeNavigation.com

I'd like to show you how to get your book published... from blank page to finished product in just 150 days.

~ Aloha Publishing Ordering Information ~

Telephone Orders: Call 208-344-2733. Have credit card ready.

Postal Orders: Aloha Publishing
                   1810 W. State Street, Suite 431
                   Boise, ID 83702

PLEASE SEND THE FOLLOWING BOOKS:

I understand that I may return any of them, for any reason, no questions asked.

Product	Price	Qty.	Subtotal
Don't Miss Your Boat: Living Your Life with Purpose in the Real World	$12.95	____	_____
Your Exceptional Life Begins Now	$14.95	____	_____
Blank to Book: From Idea to Amazon in 150 Days Manual plus one hour consultation	$97.00	____	_____

Postage: Please add $2 per product

Total Postage: $ _____

Subtotal: $ _____

Grand Total: $ _____

PLEASE CONTACT US ABOUT:

❏ Other Books   ❏ Speaking/Seminars   ❏ Coaching

Ship To: (please print)

Name: _____

Address: _____

City: _____ State: _____ Zip: _____

Phone: _____ E-mail: _____

Payment:

❏ VISA   ❏ MC   ❏ Discover   ❏ Check (payable to Aloha Publishing)

Card Number: _____

Name on Card: _____ Exp. Date: _____

Signature: _____

Please send this form along with your check or credit card information to:
Aloha Publishing
1810 W. State Street, Suite 431
Boise, ID 83702

Your Exceptional Life Begins Now
QUICK ORDER FORM

Telephone Orders: Call 208-344-2733.
Have credit card ready.

Postal Orders: Aloha Publishing
                           1810 W. State Street, Suite 431
                           Boise, ID 83702

PLEASE SEND THE FOLLOWING BOOKS:

I understand that I may return any of them, for any reason, no questions asked.

Product	Price	Qty.	Subtotal
Your Exceptional Life Begins Now SINGLE COPIES	$14.95	____	_____
Your Exceptional Life Begins Now 5-9 COPIES	$10.95	____	_____
Your Exceptional Life Begins Now 10 + COPIES	$9.95	____	_____

Postage: Single Copies Add $2.00 per book
                Quantity orders, 10+ add $1.00 per book   Total Postage: $ _____

Subtotal: $ _____

Grand Total: $ _____

PLEASE CONTACT US ABOUT:

☐ Other Books   ☐ Speaking/Seminars   ☐ Coaching

Ship To: (please print)

Name: _____

Address: _____

City: _____ State: _____ Zip: _____

Phone:_____ E-mail:_____

Payment:

☐ VISA   ☐ MC   ☐ Discover   ☐ Check (payable to Aloha Publishing)

Card Number: _____

Name on Card: _____ Exp. Date: _____

Signature: _____

Please send this form along with your check or credit card information to:

Aloha Publishing
1810 W. State Street, Suite 431
Boise, ID 83702